D1172837

SAMUEL JOHNSON

Life of Savage

SAMUEL JOHNSON

Life of Savage

EDITED BY

CLARENCE TRACY

OXFORD

AT THE CLARENDON PRESS

1971

Oxford University Press, Ely House, London W.1

GLASGOW NEW YORK TORONTO MELBOURNE WELLINGTON
CAPE TOWN SALISBURY IBADAN NAIROBI DAR ES SALAAM LUSAKA ADDIS ABABA
BOMBAY CALCUTTA MADRAS KARACHI LAHORE DACCA
KUALA LUMPUR SINGAPORE HONG KONG TOKYO

PRINTED IN GREAT BRITAIN

ACKNOWLEDGEMENTS

I owe special debts of gratitude to Professor Frederick W. Hilles of Yale University, on whom I have made many and varied demands during the last twelve years, to Professor Donald Greene of the University of Southern California, who has long shared with me an enthusiasm for Johnson's *Life of Savage*, and to Dr. J. D. Fleeman of Pembroke College, Oxford, whose expert knowledge of Johnsonian bibliography has often been put at my disposal. I am also indebted to a host of other friends and professional colleagues whose brains I have not hesitated to pick from time to time and who have always cheerfully given me help.

Financially I am indebted to the Department of External Affairs (Canada), which, on the nomination of the Royal Society of Canada, generously gave me a fellowship in 1957–8 that enabled me to spend a year in England, when the collations and other basic work on this edition were mainly done. For smaller but most welcome grants I am also indebted to the University of Saskatchewan and the University of British Columbia.

I am also indebted to the University of Glasgow for allowing me to examine and quote from the copy of Johnson's *Life of Savage* in their Euing Collection (press-mark BD20–i.41) that has some *marginalia* in Johnson's hand.

CLARENCE TRACY

Acadia University
Wolfville, Nova Scotia

CONTENTS

CONTENTS

ABBREVIATIONS

AB
The Artificial Bastard: A Biography of Richard Savage, by Clarence Tracy (Toronto, 1953).

Anonymous *Life*
THE LIFE OF MR. RICHARD SAVAGE. Who was Condemn'd with Mr. *James Gregory*, the last Sessions at the Old Baily, for the Murder of Mr. *James Sinclair*, at *Robinson*'s Coffee-house at *Charing-Cross*. 1727.

Boswell, *Life*
Boswell's Life of Johnson, ed. George Birkbeck Hill, revised by L. F. Powell, 6 vols. (Oxford, 1934–50).

GM.
Gentleman's Magazine. (Reference is made in this way: *GM*. 53. 491 = page 491 of the volume for 1753.)

INTRODUCTION

In 1743, when Johnson announced his plan to write the life of Richard Savage, he was already the author of several biographies. But there is little in them to show that he had yet conceived that theory of biography familiar to us from his essays and conversational pronouncements on the subject. For the most part they were mere digests of other books, spiced with Johnsonian commentary. But the *Account of the Life of Mr. Richard Savage* is a perfect exemplification of his theory, and, if one accepts literally his statement that nobody can write a good biography who has not eaten and drunk and lived in social intercourse with the subject of it,[1] it is almost his only good one. Nobody in his senses, of course, would deny the merits of the others, especially the mature wisdom and sound judgement that went into the *Lives of the Poets*, but none of them quite corresponds with his own theory or equals the *Life of Savage* as a personal document.

For these earlier lives Johnson ordinarily had been content with a single printed source, but for the *Life of Savage* he had several sources, enough to justify the warning he gave to possible rivals that 'it is not credible that they can obtain the same Materials'.[2] Of these the most important was the knowledge that came from personal acquaintance. Though he was ten or twelve years younger than Savage, and though they were able to associate together for only a little over a year, their acquaintance was intimate. They used to prowl about the streets together at night when they had nowhere else to go, talking politics, and to lie down to sleep in the warm ashes outside a glass factory. This

[1] Boswell, *Life*, ii. 166.
[2] *GM*. 43. 416.

intimacy is reflected in the biography, even though Johnson chose to conceal himself under the disguises of 'a Friend' and 'the Author of this Narrative', and we can see him moving about among the company, taking part in the conversation, and smiling with or at his friend as he noted everything in his memory. In the early pages, for example, he told us that Savage 'always spoke with Respect' of his schoolmaster, a remark reminiscent of long evenings of good talk, and a few pages later, rather irrelevantly, he repeated two of Savage's yarns about Steele. He implied also that Savage must have frequently talked about his trial for murder. Johnson's material of this sort naturally became richer as he went on, until he reached the time of their first meeting, in 1738, when he wrote an extended sketch of Savage's personality and mode of life. From there on, Johnson was able to record many of those 'volatile and evanescent' impressions that, as he wrote elsewhere, give vividness to biography and lead us into the 'domestick privacies . . . and minute details of daily life'.[3]

He must have soaked up much of his knowledge of Savage unconsciously, because there is no evidence of his having formed the plan to write a biography until after Savage left London for ever in 1739. Consequently Johnson did not cross-examine him as Boswell might have done. If he had, he would have been able to write a better account than he did of Savage's early life, correcting errors in his principal documentary source, the anonymous *Life* of 1727, that, unknown to him, Savage had set right in a letter to Elizabeth Carter. Johnson might also have been able to expand the weak middle section of his book, for which he had few anecdotes and no documentary sources except Savage's works, and avoid blunders like the disastrous one over the date of the *Bastard* that not only threw out the order of events but also led him to make unwarranted deduc-

---

[3] *Rambler,* no. 60 (Saturday, 13 Oct. 1750).

tions as to the motives of both Savage and his patron, Lord Tyrconnel. Moreover, even after he had announced his intention to write a biography, he failed to interview many of Savage's surviving friends and relatives. Pope, who was ill and dying, he never met, though he may have received some information from him indirectly and sometimes wrote as if he knew more about Pope's actions and feelings than he was free to publish. So far as we know, he made no approaches to either Lady Mason or Lady Macclesfield (now Mrs. Brett), and might not have learned much from them even if he had done so. But he would have found willing talkers in Aaron Hill, Thomas Birch, James Thomson, and David Mallet, who had known Savage longer than he had. Benjamin Victor, another of Savage's old friends, mentioned his willingness in a letter to John Dyer when he heard what Johnson was about: 'if the author would enrich, and enliven his work, he should come to you, and I, for anecdotes.'[4] Dyer was in Hereford at the time, but honest, easy-going, conversable Victor was close by. As a biographer Johnson never had Boswell's eager curiosity for facts, and relied more than Boswell did on his own insights.[5]

He did, however, make some inquiries and even got information from sources outside London. Though he learned little about Savage's life in Wales, the pages describing his life in Bristol are full and lively. Johnson, poor and busy as he was, could hardly have gone there himself to collect information, and it is equally unlikely that his employer, Edward Cave, had taken that trouble. The Bristol bookseller Thomas Cadell, however, appears to have been Cave's correspondent there, and, though the Savage manuscript that he sent to Cave in 1749 arrived too late, he may very well have earlier sent Johnson the information that he

---

[4] Benjamin Victor, *Original Letters* (1776), i. 68.

[5] Cf. Boswell, *Life*, iii. 344–5: JOHNSON, 'If it rained knowledge I'd hold out my hand; but I would not give myself the trouble to go in quest of it.' Cf. *University of Toronto Quarterly*, xv (1945–6), 86–93.

did use.[6] Someone, indeed, must have transmitted facts about Savage's habits that Savage himself would not have reported, such as his annoying his friends there by staying in their homes until all hours and his gradually being frozen out of Bristol society, and must have interviewed Mr. Dagge, the 'tender Goaler', who alone could have contributed the anecdotes about Savage's life in prison, his illness, and his last words. For these closing pages Johnson's anecdotal material was copious, and yet none of it could have been first-hand.

In addition to anecdotes, Johnson used letters written by Savage to London friends after his departure in 1739, especially during his imprisonment in Bristol when he had much leisure for the purpose, though it is hard to identify them because of Johnson's practice of either paraphrasing them or quoting mere scraps without mentioning the names of recipients, or dates and addresses. Johnson may also have been in possession of papers left behind by Savage when he quitted the city, such as the text of Savage's lampoon on Miller, which he must have had though he did not print it,[7] the speech of Mr. Justice Page, which can be found in none of the extant accounts of Savage's trial,[8] and the epigram on Dennis, which he may have thought to have been by Savage because he found it in a manuscript copy in Savage's hand.[9] Those three were all short enough for him to have retained them only in his capacious memory, but that he had them in manuscript seems more likely. Finally, he had the manuscript of Savage's last poem, 'London and Bristol Delineated', which Savage had sent from Bristol to Cave for publication.

The remainder of his materials were printed documents, and for the first time in his career as a biographer he assembled a number of them, often overlapping and sometimes contradictory, and managed them with scholarly skill,

[6] Cf. *Poetical Works of Richard Savage*, ed. Clarence Tracy (Cambridge, 1962), p. 9 n.

[7] pp. 100–1.   [8] p. 34.   [9] p. 50.

carefully weighing one against another in a conscientious attempt to arrive at an impartial and well-balanced story. The bulk of these were provided by Cave; for when Johnson was paid for his work, he signed a receipt for fifteen guineas 'in full', as the document specified, 'for compiling and writing the Life of Richd Savage Esq. deceased and in full for all materials thereto applyed and not found by the said Edward Cave'.[10] What Cave handed over to him at the outset is not recorded, but it must have included, in addition to the poem just mentioned and the correspondence relating to it, two printed accounts of Savage's early life: the anonymous *Life of Mr. Richard Savage* printed in 1727 and Giles Jacob's *Poetical Register* (1719), which contained a two-page article on him. Later Johnson wrote to Cave asking him for further materials: 'Towards Mr Savage's Life what more have you got? I would willingly have his tryal &c and know whether his Defence be at Bristol, and would have his Collection of Poems on account of the Preface—the Plain Dealer—All the Magazins that have anything of his or relating to him.'[11] Evidently Cave responded to this request, because, with the exception of the 'defence', Johnson was able to use all of them: the files of the *Gentleman's Magazine* and the *Plain Dealer*, Savage's *Miscellaneous Poems*, and a printed account of his trial for murder. In addition to those, Johnson got from somebody copies of many of Savage's separately printed poems.

Johnson's request for further material bearing on Savage's trial shows that he was fully aware of the need for verifying his facts. He already possessed a lengthy account of it in the anonymous *Life*, but he must have felt that it was biased. So he asked for the 'tryal'. What he got is not certain. There were at least three catchpenny accounts of it—*The Proceedings at Justice Hall*, *The Old Bailey Sessions Papers*, and

[10] Boswell, *Life*, i. 165 n.
[11] *Letters of Samuel Johnson*, ed. R. W. Chapman (Oxford, 1952), i. 21.

Select Trials; but since they are almost identical in their reports of Savage's trial, one cannot be sure which of them Johnson used. Some of the details he mentioned, however, can have come only from one of them: the rude and aggressive behaviour of Savage and his party; Merchant's having given the provocation by rushing into the room where the brawl occurred, monopolizing the fire, and kicking over a table; and, after the crime had been committed, Savage's turning pale and acting in a bewildered manner—these came from evidence given by witnesses for the prosecution. Johnson had also asked for Savage's 'defence'. He may have meant manuscript notes made by Savage for his own use in the conduct of his case, but probably no such document existed, and we hear nothing about it in the *Life*. But somehow Johnson managed to give far more space and emphasis to the defendants' case than had either the anonymous *Life* or *Select Trials*. The final argument of the defence mentioned by Johnson—'that neither Reason nor Law obliged a Man to wait for the Blow which was threatened, and which, if he should suffer it, he might never be able to return'—and Savage's admission of guilt are not to be found in any of the printed sources. Whatever Johnson's authority for those statements may have been, his account of the episode is a remarkable piece of biographical reconstruction.

Some critics, however, have been less struck by Johnson's objectivity than by a desire to whitewash Savage. Certainly Johnson's opinion of him was high. He called him 'the Man of exalted Sentiments, extensive Views and curious Observations, the Man whose Remarks on Life might have assisted the Statesman, whose Ideas of Virtue might have enlightened the Moralist, whose Eloquence might have influenced Senates, and whose Delicacy might have polished Courts'. A page or two might easily be filled with other flattering things said by Johnson about both the man and his poems. These superlatives are overdone, but we would not be so much struck by them if we read them as they were first published, in a detached biography rather than in the context of the *Lives of the Poets*, a work of which the characteristic tone is that of judicial appraisal. Of course, exaggeration sometimes broke through even in the *Lives of the Poets*; for Johnson's hills were generally mountains rather than considerable protruberances; but in them his more characteristic form of extravagance was negative. He loved to prick people's critical bubbles, and offended many of his readers by his adverse comments on Milton. The consequence of reading the *Life of Savage* in that context is that Johnson appears to have been praising Savage more highly than Milton—a preposterous impression, far indeed from what he must have meant to give, for between the two works lay some thirty-five years with all the personal and intellectual development that they had brought him. One has to put away from one's mind the images of the Great Cham and the national oracle, and remember instead the anonymous young author, conscious of extraordinary powers and eager to make his reputation. Actuated by a generous desire to shield the memory of his friend from malevolent criticism, he was youthful, urgent, and warm. He felt that he could best serve his friend by telling the whole truth; and it is easy to make allowances for his exaggerations if we read the *Life* by itself, away from the incongruous company in which it has been put.

That it was the whole truth he wanted to tell appears in his awareness of the weaknesses in Savage's character. At their first meeting Johnson had been struck by the contrast between his noble ideals and his childlike irresponsibility. This was implied in his Latin epigram marking the beginning of their acquaintance:

> Humani studium generis qui pectore fervet,
> O! colat humanum Te foveatque genus![12]

[12] *GM*. 38. 210.

(Devotion to mankind burns in your breast! O! may mankind in turn cherish and protect you!) That antithesis rings through his book. He scarcely ever mentioned one of Savage's merits without afterwards balancing it with a weakness, or mentioned a weakness without balancing it with a merit. Often the weaknesses were venial ones about which Johnson could feel both amusement and disapproval. Obviously, for example, he had had little sympathy with Savage's plan to escape from his troubles by flying into Wales, and he himself must have been the friend who 'gently reproach'd' him 'for submitting to live upon a Subscription' and advised him 'by a resolute Exertion of his Abilities to support himself'. Johnson also had been amused by Savage's delusions regarding country life, about which Savage had no information except, as Johnson said, 'from Pastorals and Songs', especially his belief that 'the Melody of the Nightingale', which was to be heard 'from every Bramble', was 'a very important Part of the Happiness of a Country Life'. Knowing how Johnson felt about the country, we can only admire his restraint. His attitude was much the same towards the hubbub Savage stirred up over the tactlessness of his benefactors, who, instead of allowing him to select his own clothes, had sent a tailor to measure him. Johnson observed his 'violent Agonies of Rage' with mingled sympathy and astonishment, and contrived to convey his feeling that the whole thing was absurd by one of his most skilful anticlimaxes. He could never bring himself, he said, to ask Savage 'how the Affair ended, for fear of renewing his Uneasiness'. Sympathy and a sense of the ridiculous went hand in hand.

Sometimes, however, Johnson was sarcastic, as in his remark that Savage had 'taken Care' to make known in coffee-houses all over London his support of the party in opposition and his admiration for Lord Bolingbroke. The reason for that rebuke was that Savage owed his life to the mercy of the Government and had been supported for years on a pension paid by the Queen. Moreover Savage's writing a satire on Bristol while in prison there, and his insistence on acknowledging his authorship of it even though he knew that the hostility created would destroy his last hope of release, had also struck Johnson as ungrateful and unwise. He gave the facts as objectively as he could, and then broke out with amazement:

> Such was his Imprudence and such his obstinate Adherence to his own Resolutions, however absurd. A Prisoner! supported by Charity! and, whatever Insults he might have received during the latter Part of his Stay in *Bristol*, once caressed, esteemed, and presented with a liberal Collection, he could forget on a sudden his Danger, and his Obligations, to gratify the Petulance of his Wit, or the Eagerness of his Resentment.

Those barbed shafts were certainly not uncalled for, and must dispel any lingering belief that Johnson had swallowed Savage whole.

Johnson's outstanding impression of Savage, indeed, seems to have been the paradox of the man: a genius capable of enlightening statesmen, but lacking the common sense of a schoolboy; a moralist of high principle, who had committed most of the seven deadly sins; an accomplished gentleman who had moved easily in the best society, but who never had had a home of his own and commonly slept in fetid night-cellars among the most depraved of mankind. In him Johnson had had under observation one of the strangest, most fascinating, and most revealing specimens of human nature that any biographer ever dealt with. He drew together the disparate elements in Savage by balancing them one against the other, and in the end welded them into a symbol, the embodiment of those cardinal sins that he constantly warned his readers against: day-dreaming, self-deception, self-dramatization, and self-pity. Savage was not a man who meant ill, but he was one who did ill, because he for ever applied to himself the opiates of self-deception, and was always satisfied with himself. Thus the *Life of Savage* became a cautionary tale in which Johnson solemnly asserted that 'this Relation will not be wholly without its Use, if those, who languish under any Part of his Sufferings, shall be enabled to fortify their Patience. . . .' But it was saved from sinking to the usual level of an improving work by its author's insight into character and his skill in its portrayal. Above all it was saved by the fact that Johnson had loved Savage and, without forgetting or condoning his sins, had continued to love him to the end.

TEXTUAL INTRODUCTION

Symbol

44   AN | ACCOUNT | OF THE | LIFE | OF | Mr
Richard Savage, | Son of the Earl Rivers. | [ornament] | *LONDON:* | Printed for J. Roberts in
Warwick-Lane. | M.DCC.XLIV.

    8° (4s): A^2 B–2A^4 2B^2, pp. *i*[*–ii*] half-title, *iii*[*–iv*] title,
12–184, 179–80 *text*, *187* advt., *188* blank.

    There are two states: copies of the second have the
following erratum on the last page of the text: 'P. 77.
l. 9. *read* would NOT substract.'

    Copies consulted: first state: Yale (x2), Bodleian,
Gwyn Jones, the editor; Second state: Yale (x2).

    The copy belonging to the editor has provided the
copy-text of this edition.

48   AN | ACCOUNT | OF THE | LIFE | OF | Mr
Richard Savage, | Son of the Earl Rivers. | [rule] |
The Second Edition. | [rule] | *LONDON:* |
Printed for E. Cave at *St John's Gate.* | M.DCC.
XLVIII.

    8° (4s): A^2 B–2A^4 2B^2, pp. *i*[*–ii*] half-title, *iii*[*–iv*] title,
12–184, 179–80 *text*, *187-8* blank.

    A reprint of 44 with extensive revision.
Copies consulted: Bodleian, Ralph Williams, F. W.
Hilles, the editor.

67   THE | LIFE | OF | Mr. Richard Savage, | SON
of the Earl RIVERS. | The THIRD EDITION. |
To which are added, | The LIVES of | Sir
FRANCIS DRAKE, | AND | ADMIRAL
BLAKE. | All Written by the fame Author. |

*Reprints published in Dublin have not been used in constituting this text.

[parallel rule] | *LONDON:* | Printed for HENRY and CAVE, at St. John's Gate. | M.DCC.LXVII. 12°. *A*² B–N¹² O⁶, *i*[–*ii*] title, i–ii Preface, 1–172 Savage, 173–272 Drake, 273–98 Blake, *299–300* advts.

A reprint of 48. The author is identified in the Preface as 'the ingenious Author of the *Rambler*'. His authorship, however, had been publicly mentioned previously. *GM.* 53. 491–2.

Reissued in 1769 with a cancel-title reading as follows: THE | LIFE | OF | MR. RICHARD SAVAGE, | SON of the EARL RIVERS. | The FOURTH EDITION. | To which are added, | The LIVES of | SIR FRANCIS DRAKE, | AND | ADMIRAL BLAKE. | All written by the AUTHOR of the RAMBLER. | [parallel rule] | LONDON, | Printed for F. NEWBERY, at the Corner of St. Paul's | Church Yard, Ludgate Street. | M.DCC.LXIX.

Reissued again in 1775 with a cancel-title reading as follows: THE | LIFE | OF | Mr. RICHARD SAVAGE, | SON of the EARL RIVERS. | The FOURTH EDITION. | To which are added, | The LIVES of | SIR FRANCIS DRAKE, | AND | ADMIRAL BLAKE. | All WRITTEN by the AUTHOR OF THE RAMBLER. | [parallel rule] | LONDON: | Printed for F. NEWBERY, at the Corner of St. Paul's | Church-Yard. | 1775.

Copies consulted: First issue: University of Saskatchewan, Bodleian, British Museum; Second issue: Bodleian; Third issue: University of Rochester.

75   THE | WORKS | OF | RICHARD SAVAGE, ESQ. | SON OF | THE EARL RIVERS. | WITH AN ACCOUNT OF THE | LIFE AND WRITINGS OF THE AUTHOR, | BY SAMUEL JOHNSON, LL. D. | IN TWO VOLUMES. | VOL. I. [–II.] | [engraved vignette] | LONDON: |

PRINTED FOR T. EVANS IN THE STRAND. | M DCC LXXV.

8º. I: π^2 a*^{2} a–g^8 h^2 A–L^8 M^6, pp. i[–ii] half-title, iii[–iv] title, v–$viii$ Dedication, i–iii iv–cxvi *Life of Savage*, i ii–iv, 5 6–187, Works, 188 blank. II: π^2 A–R^8 S^2, pp. i[–ii] half title, iii[–iv] title, i ii–vi, 7 8–271 text, 272–76 Contents &c.

A reprint of 44 with extensive cuts in the quoted matter.

Copies consulted: Bodleian, the editor.

77a THE | LIFE | OF | Mr. RICHARD SAVAGE, | SON of the EARL RIVERS. | THE FOURTH EDITION. | TO WHICH ARE ADDED, | THE LIVES OF | SIR FRANCIS DRAKE, | AND | ADMIRAL BLAKE. | All written by the Author of the RAMBLER. | [parallel rule] | LONDON: | Printed for F. NEWBERY, the Corner of St. Paul's | Church-Yard. 1777.

12º. A^2 B–N^{12} O^6, contents as for 67. A reprint of 67.

Copies consulted: University of Saskatchewan, the editor.

77b THE | WORKS | OF | RICHARD SAVAGE, | ESQ. | SON OF | THE EARL RIVERS. | WITH AN ACCOUNT OF THE | LIFE AND WRIT- INGS OF THE AUTHOR, | BY SAMUEL JOHNSON, LL. D. | A NEW EDITION. | VOL. I. [–II.] | [engraved vignette] | LONDON: | PRINTED FOR T. EVANS IN THE STRAND. | M DCC LXXVII.

8º. I: π^4 a–g^8 h^2 A–L^8 M^4 N^2, contents as for 75; II: π^2 A–R^8 S^6, pp. i[–ii] half-title, iii[–iv] title, i ii–vi, 7 8–279 text, 280–284 Contents &c.

A reprint of 75.

Copies consulted: Bodleian, the editor.

79–81* PREFACES, | BIOGRAPHICAL | AND | CRITICAL, | TO THE | WORKS | OF THE | ENGLISH POETS. | BY SAMUEL JOHN- SON. | [short spread rule] | VOLUME THE NINTH. | [short spread rule] | LONDON: | PRINTED BY J. NICHOLS; | [ten lines of book- sellers' names] | M DCC LXXXI.

8°. a² b–k⁸ l² A⁴, ²A–B⁸ C⁴, ³A⁶, ⁴A⁸. pp. *i*[*–ii*] general title, *iii*[*–iv*] half-title, 1–147, *148* Savage, 1–7, *8* Somervile, 1–40 Thomson, 1–11, *12* Hammond, 1–14, *15*–16 Collins.

A reprint of 75.

Copies consulted: Bodleian, Yale, University of Saskat- chewan, the editor.

81 THE | LIVES | OF THE MOST EMINENT | ENGLISH POETS; | WITH | CRITICAL OBSERVATIONS | ON THEIR | WORKS. | By SAMUEL JOHNSON. | [short spread rule] | VOLUME III | [short spread rule] | LONDON: | [eight lines of booksellers' names] | MDCCLXXXI.

8°. a² B–2G⁸, pp. *i*[*–ii*] title, *iii*[*–iv*] Contents, *1–2*, *3–462*, *463–64* text.

A reprint of 79–81.

Copies consulted: Bodleian, the editor.

83 THE | LIVES | OF THE MOST EMINENT | ENGLISH POETS; | WITH | CRITICAL OBSERVATIONS | ON THEIR | WORKS. | By SAMUEL JOHNSON. | A NEW EDITION, CORRECTED. | [short spread rule] | THE THIRD VOLUME. | [short spread rule] |

---

* The first four of the ten volumes constituting this edition were pub- lished in 1779.

LONDON: [eight lines of booksellers' names] |
M DCC LXXXIII.

8⁰. *A*² B–G⁸ H⁸(H6+ '*H7'.1) I–2E⁸, pp. *i*[*–ii*] title,
iii[*–iv*] Contents, 1–432 text.

A reprint of 81 with a few corrections to the text
of *Savage*.

Copies consulted: Bodleian, Yale, University of Saskatchewan.

DESCENT OF THE TEXT

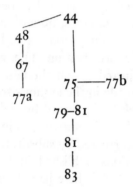

No part of the manuscript of Johnson's life of Savage
having survived, the earliest source of the text is the edition
printed for Roberts by Cave in 1744, which provides the
copy-text for this new edition. Begun in the summer of
1743, the manuscript was not finished until 14 December,
when the author was paid off.[1] Though this was a long time
for a rapid writer like Johnson to have been at work on a

---

[1] Boswell, *Life*, i. 165 n.

narrative of less than 200 octavo pages, he was always inter-
mittent in his habits of work and at this time had other things
to do. The style is colloquial, and, as Robert Potter wrote in
1789, 'he rather talks than writes'.[2] The author himself remarked that he 'wrote forty-eight of the printed octavo
pages . . . at a sitting',[3] and there are signs of hasty composition. In later editions he made changes, most of them
correcting infelicities of style, such as repetitions of the
same word, redundancies, and tangled syntax. In the present
edition, except for obvious misprints, no attempt has been
made to correct the text where Johnson himself never
corrected it. The copy-text has been reproduced with its
accidentals intact, except that f has been changed to s,
catchwords have been omitted, quotation marks have been
dropped from centred quotations as well as running ones
from quotations of more than one line, and cues for footnotes have been adjusted to suit the new layout. No other
changes have been made in the author's treatment of quotations, some of which he indicated by italics and others by
quotation marks.[4] In substantive readings, however, the
copy-text has been corrected by substituting authorial readings from later editions published in London during his
lifetime, especially 48. All these have been recorded in the
Textual Notes.

Before we examine Johnson's revisions, however, a special
problem must be dealt with. Though he said that he did not
consider it his 'Province' to 'display' the beauties of Savage's
works,[5] he included enough extracts from them to make up
an anthology. This was clearly intended to be a special
feature of his book; in the advertisement of it in the *General*

---

[2] *The Art of Criticism; as Exemplified in Dr. Johnson's Lives* (1789),
p. 123.
[3] Boswell, *Life*, v. 67; cf. J. D. Fleeman, *Library*, xxii (1967), 341–52.
[4] Johnson used italics indiscriminately for both direct and indirect
quotations.
[5] p. 54.

Evening Post for 25 August 1743 he made a point of his
plan to give the world the text of the then unpublished poem
'London and Bristol Delineated'.[6] Evidently he had once
intended also to include one of Aaron Hill's *Plain Dealers*,
because on page 12 a footnote read: '*Plain Dealer*. See
Appendix.' (There was, however, no appendix, and in the
next edition the words referring to it disappeared.) All together these quotations make up a considerable part of his
book. A few of them, like 'London and Bristol Delineated',
were printed from manuscript copies, probably in Savage's
hand, and one or two others may have been written down
from memory, but the majority came from printed sources,
mainly the books supplied to Johnson by Cave.[7] For these,
of course, we have a text earlier and more authoritative than
the edition of 1744. The policy adopted by the present
editor regarding them grows out of a recognition of the fact
that they fall into two groups that Johnson himself treated
differently. For most of the longer quotations he apparently
sent printed copies, suitably marked and edited,[8] to the
printer, who set type directly from them. Such appear to be
the Preface to *Miscellaneous Poems*,[9] the Dedication to the
'Author to be Let',[10] three long passages from the *Wanderer*,[11]
one from 'Of Public Spirit',[12] several extracts from the

---

[6] Quoted in J. L. Clifford, *Young Sam Johnson* (New York, 1955),
pp. 273–4. Johnson was anticipated by M. Cooper, who brought out an
edition of the poem in Dec. 1743.

[7] Boswell, *Life*, i. 156.

[8] Johnson must have marked the beginnings and endings of the extracts
to be printed as well as any omissions. The latter are usually, but not
always, indicated in the text by dashes. He did relatively little other
editing, but he did omit the signature 'T. B.' from the end of the letter
quoted from the *Gentleman's Magazine* on p. 76, believing that the real
author of it was Savage not Thomas Birch. Moreover, when the ensuing
poem was omitted in the edition of 1775, changes were also made in the
text of the letter itself, regardless of the fact that the words emended
were Savage's (or Birch's), not Johnson's.

[9] pp. 27–9 n.

[10] pp. 46–9 n.

[11] pp. 54–8 n.

[12] p. 93 n.

Gentleman's Magazine,[13] and perhaps others. These all show a high degree of accuracy, such errors as do occur being the result of Johnson's failure to read proof. Though a few corrections were made in them in later editions, no systematic revision was ever made. Consequently, in the present edition the substantive readings in the quotations mentioned have been corrected by means of the printed texts that the printer used, which have the authority usually recognized in a manuscript, and all such corrections have been recorded in the Textual Notes. The remaining quotations, all of them shorter ones, must have been either written down from memory or transcribed by Johnson from printed copies that it was not convenient to send to the printer. The number of inaccuracies is great, but in every case the result makes sense, usually much the same sense as the original. Some of these changes may even have been deliberate: for example, a brief quotation from the *Wanderer* is made to read, 'I fly all public Care . . .', whereas Savage had written, 'She [i.e. his muse] flies all public Care'.[14] In the present edition, consequently, Johnson's readings in these quotations have not been corrected, since they are not the blunders of a compositor but the products of his own mind and hence a real part of *his* text. The proper readings, however, have been recorded in the Textual Notes.

The second edition, printed in 1748 by Edward Cave, is the most important one after the first. Derived from a copy of the first edition containing the erratum notice, in appearance and accidentals it resembles it closely, and in many places is a careful line-by-line reprint. Its importance comes from the fact that its text had undergone a systematic revision, more than eighty substantive changes having been made, mainly affecting the style. Most of them must have been made by Johnson, and even the doubtful ones, that might have been made by a compositor, gain authority from

[13] pp. 41–2 n., 42 n., 76–9, 85 n., 88–9 n., and 89–91 n.
[14] p. 52.

our knowledge of the care with which the author looked over the whole text. He never did so again. Consequently 48 is our prime authority for substantive readings in the text as a whole. Except where Johnson did make further revisions later, all substantive changes other than obvious errors have been incorporated in this edition.

In 48, however, Johnson made few changes in the facts he mentioned, and it is remarkable that he made none in what he wrote about Savage's relations with Pope. Readers of the first edition must have been struck by the fact that although Johnson wrote that Pope had been 'a steady and unalienable Friend' to Savage 'almost to the End of his Life',[15] his name did not occur except in marginal and innocuous contexts. When writing about Savage's involvement in the *Dunciad*, or about Pope's raising a fund for Savage's support, or about their quarrel, Johnson sidestepped it. Pressure must have been brought to bear by Pope, who was embarrassed over his connection with Savage, either on Johnson or his printer to mention him as little as possible. Dr. Fleeman has conjectured that when the last 48 pages of the first edition were withdrawn and rewritten, it was in order to allow Johnson either to add something or suppress something, and in either case he suggests that the subject was Pope.[16] Admittedly there is little positive evidence to support his conjecture, but the fact is significant that the rewriting began just at the point at which he had much to say about Pope and where he might have been expected to mention him by name frequently. By 1748, however, not only was Pope dead but the story of his relations with Savage had been made public by William Ayre in his two-volume *Memoirs of the Life and Writings of Alexander Pope, Esq.* (1745). Ayre devoted over thirty

---

[15] p. 51. Pope's name, however, is mentioned frequently in some of the matter quoted from Savage in the notes.
[16] Op. cit.

pages of his second volume to the story, most of it stolen
from Johnson, often word for word. But, unlike Johnson,
he introduced Pope's name many times. He added little new
information, but he did completely remove the veil of
secrecy that had up to then hung over Pope's part in Savage's
biography. Johnson's continued silence about it is hard to
account for on any grounds other than his feeling bound by
a promise or by his respect for Pope's known wishes.

At some time after 1748, however, Johnson must have
thought once more, if only transiently, of revising his text
and, among other things, incorporating the Pope material.
The copy of the second edition reported by Dr. Fleeman
in Glasgow contains notes and corrections in Johnson's
hand.[17] Though it is a sophisticated copy, containing sheets
C, D, E, G, L, and O from the first edition, Johnson's notes
occur only on sheets belonging to the second edition,
actually in two widely separated parts of the book, at the
beginning and at the end, viz. sheet B and sheets S, T, U,
Z, 2A, and 2B. If Johnson's notes were made on the sheets
before they were bound up, it is possible that he had also
made notes on other sheets that were somehow lost and
replaced in the bound book by ones from the first edition;
but, judging from the book as it stands, one can only say
that his effort at revision was neither sustained nor systematic, and that it probably was the work of only a few
minutes. It is impossible to be sure when it occurred.
Several of the jottings in sheet T and subsequently refer to
Pope, two of them reflecting footnotes added in 1775,[18]
and another an addition made to the text only in 1783. It
seems likely that Johnson was toying with the thought of
incorporating information about Pope that he needed no
longer to keep quiet. In this edition all the emendations
made in the Glasgow copy, substantive and accidental,

[17] Op. cit.
[18] pp. 112 and 134.

have been incorporated into the text, and all Johnson's jottings included in the explanatory notes.[19]

The text of 48 was used as it stood for the third edition (1767) and, in turn, handed down to Newbery's reprint of it (1777). Although Johnson evidently did not give the text as close attention as he had done previously, there are between forty and fifty substantive variants, several of which were most likely authorial, such as the addition of the words '*Anno* 1743' in one place,[20] as well as a number of stylistic changes that often sound Johnsonian, though they were not necessarily made by him. Many of the changes, however, like the removal of a hypergrammatical 'If' in another place,[21] might have been made by any competent compositor, others are 'improvements' that Johnson probably would not have relished, and a few are downright blunders. Nevertheless 67, though falling far short of 48 in authority, is superior to most of its successors. Newbery's reprint of it in 1777 was textually careless but deserves some respect because it is the last edition to retain Johnson's revisions of 1748.

Meanwhile, in 1775, the *Life* was incorporated as an introduction in a two-volume collection of Savage's works published by Thomas Evans. Nothing is known about the circumstances in which this was produced or about any connection subsisting at this time between Evans and Johnson; but it is a reasonable assumption that this use of his work had Johnson's approval, because the text established in 1775 was later used as it stood in the *Prefaces, Biographical and Critical* (1779–81), Evans being one of the syndicate that published that work under an agreement with Johnson.[22] Evans, who, according to his obituary notice in

---

[19] Textual revisions are largely confined to sheet B. Later notes are mainly explanatory or even reminiscent.

[20] p. 39.

[21] p. 46.

[22] His name appears on the title-page of 79–81.

the *Gentleman's Magazine*, ' had naturally a taste and a love for literature',[23] was the editor of Savage's works, signing a footnote on page 172 of the second volume with his initial, E, and most likely considered himself also the editor of Johnson's biography, taking on himself the responsibility for carrying out changes that Johnson must have sanctioned. Unfortunately he chose 44 as his copy-text, even using a copy lacking the erratum. Either Johnson was not consulted over the choice, or had himself forgotten the revisions made in 1748, which were consequently lost sight of; for 75 is the ancestor of all later editions (except 77a) almost to our own time. The changes that Evans made were extensive. For the first time the *Life* was ceasing to be a separate work and becoming a preface; consequently most of the lengthy and now redundant quotations were cut and replaced by cross-references to the pages in the latter parts of the collection where they occurred in their original contexts. At the same time corrections were made, some of which Johnson had previously made in 48; others were corrections of errors that had escaped notice through the three earlier editions. A missing Christian name was supplied in a footnote,[24] a parenthesis was closed correctly,[25] several grammatical slips were amended, and other small blemishes were removed. Moreover, some of the quotations that were being retained were checked against Savage's printed texts and corrected; indeed, in a quotation from *The Bastard*, which Johnson had derived from Savage's revised text printed in the *Gentleman's Magazine*, a reading was altered in order to conform with that of one of the earlier separate editions.[26] Five footnotes were added, of which one supplied a year date,[27] and two others identified Pope as the person referred

[23] *GM.* 84. 396.
[24] p. 24.
[25] p. 122.
[26] p. 75.
[27] p. 135. See Textual Note.

to in the text.[28] These last are most interesting. They could hardly have been introduced entirely without Johnson's authority; and yet it is odd that, if Johnson did in fact no longer feel committed to secrecy over Pope, he did not put his name into the text itself, rather than into footnotes, and that he did not put it in wherever it belonged, rather than in just these two places. Consequently one cannot be absolutely certain that these footnotes are strictly authorial. Perhaps Johnson had given Evans *carte blanche* for minor corrections, and the latter went as far as he dared. It is impossible to be sure. There are forty variants in all, plus nine others in the reprint of 1777. The ones not already described do not win much respect for Evans's text. Some of them are careless slips, and several are gross blunders; among the latter are the alteration of 'State' to 'case',[29] of 'as long' to 'as long as',[30] and of 'others in Studies' to the quite nonsensical 'in other studies'.[31] The worst of all is the bungling attempt to correct an obvious error previously mentioned. On page 46 Johnson had undoubtedly written:

The *Author to be let* was first published in a single Pamphlet, and afterwards inserted in a Collection of Pieces relating to the *Dunciad*, which were addressed by Mr. *Savage* to the Earl of *Middlesex*, in a Dedication, which he was prevailed upon to sign, though he did not write it, and in which there are some Positions, that the true Author would perhaps not have published under his own Name; and on which Mr. *Savage* afterwards reflected with no great Satisfaction.

In 44 that sentence began with 'If', an error that remained uncorrected in 48. 67 simply dropped the 'If'. But 75, instead of making the obvious correction, changed the full stop at the end of the sentence into a semicolon, eliminated the paragraph division that followed, and ran the two sentences

[28] pp. 112, 134.
[29] p. 17.
[30] p. 103.
[31] p. 136.

together, producing a grammatical monstrosity. Johnson could not conceivably have been responsible for such a change, or have noticed it in proof. But it remained in 77b, 79–81, 81, and 83—clear evidence of the casualness with which the author supervised all these later printings. In the present edition the material Evans cut has been restored, since the work is now again a separate publication, not an introduction; but only such variants have been incorporated as seem to have valid claim to being authorial.

The *Prefaces, Biographical and Critical* (1779–81), as mentioned before, adopted Evans's 1775 text, ignoring his reprint of 1777 even though it furnished the text of Savage's poems for the corresponding volume of the *Works*. Several further cuts were made, but few authorial variants were introduced. It departed from its copy-text in twenty-six substantive places. Some of these are obvious errors, some are corrections made by a compositor of obvious errors, and others are ambivalent. A change from 'but' to 'tho' [32] revived a correction made by Johnson himself in 48; one from 'nearly' to 'narrowly' [33] is probably not authorial since according to Johnson's *Dictionary* the two words are synonymous in this sense. The alteration of 'Treatments' from plural to singular [34] is probably also not authorial since Johnson derived 'treatment' from the French, rather than from the English word 'treat', and was probably thinking of the French expression *subir de mauvais traitements*. Similarly the change in the use of the verb 'trample' [35] from transitive to intransitive is probably not authorial, even though a comparable change had been made in 67, since Johnson must have been recalling the passage in Matt. 7: 6 that he quoted under this word in the *Dictionary*. These are the most interesting of the variants in 79–81, none of which establishes a clear case for its authority.

There is even less reason for accepting as authorial any of

[32] p. 126.   [33] p. 46.   [34] p. 37.   [35] p. 99.

the readings of 81, though there are several corrections of errors that must have been made by means of reference to earlier editions, especially 48. None of the new readings introduced is certainly authorial, and most of them are obvious blunders.

But in the edition of 1783 six emendations were made, all certainly authorial. One of them requires special mention. On page 135, where Johnson wrote about Pope's quarrel with Savage, he now added two sentences that were adumbrated in one of his marginal notes in the Glasgow copy: 'Henley, in one of his advertisements, had mentioned *Pope's treatment of Savage.* This was supposed by Pope to be the consequence of a complaint made by Savage to Henley, and was therefore mentioned by him with much resentment.' Though this is certainly authorial, I have been unable to include it in the text of this edition, because, when Johnson added it, he must have forgotten that Pope's name had not previously been mentioned in this connection (except in the two footnotes cautiously added in 1775). Consequently the two new sentences are virtually incomprehensible to a reader who reads only the text and would jar even one who also reads the notes. Unless an editor were to make the changes in the earlier part of the narrative that Johnson himself seems once or twice to have contemplated but never made, it is better to consign this ill-considered addition to the explanatory notes. The other five have been incorporated in this edition.

The history of Johnson's concern for his text, then, is that he made one thorough overhaul of it in 1748 and afterwards left it alone except for tinkering with it in places from time to time, as in the Glasgow copy. It is remarkable that when it was included in the *Prefaces, Biographical and Critical* he did not cut it down to the scale of the other lives of minor poets. Dr. Fleeman has suggested to me privately that the fact that the *Savage* was not published in 1779 when the first four volumes of *Prefaces* were released, as it easily might have been, may indicate that he had the intention, later abandoned, of writing a new life of Savage. In 1781, however, the text was merely set up from an existing printed text with minor adjustments that could have been made by an employee of the printing house. Consequently there is nothing to challenge the supremacy of the first two editions.

AN
ACCOUNT

OF THE
LIFE

OF

Mr *Richard Savage,*

Son of the Earl RIVERS.

LONDON:

Printed for J. ROBERTS in *Warwick-Lane.*
M.DCC.XLIV.

AN ACCOUNT OF THE

LIFE OF

MR. RICHARD SAVAGE

It has been observed in all Ages, that the Advantages of Nature or of Fortune have contributed very little to the Promotion of Happiness; and that those whom the Splendor of their Rank, or the Extent of their Capacity, have placed upon the Summits of human Life, have not often given any just Occasion to Envy in those who look up to them from a lower Station. Whether it be that apparent Superiority incites great Designs, and great Designs are naturally liable to fatal Miscarriages, or that the general Lot of Mankind is Misery, and the Misfortunes of those whose Eminence drew upon them universal Attention, have been more carefully recorded, because they were more generally observed, and have in reality been only more conspicuous than those of others, not more frequent, or more severe.

That Affluence and Power, Advantages extrinsic and adventitious, and therefore easily separable from those by whom they are possessed, should very often flatter the Mind with Expectation of Felicity which they cannot give, raises no Astonishment; but it seems rational to hope, that intellectual Greatness should produce better Effects, that Minds qualified for great Attainments should first endeavour their own Benefit, and that they who are most able to teach others the Way to Happiness, should with most Certainty follow it themselves.

3

But this Expectation, however plausible, has been very frequently disappointed. The Heroes of literary as well as civil History have been very often no less remarkable for what they have suffered, than for what they have atchieved; and Volumes have been written only to enumerate the Miseries of the Learned, and relate their unhappy Lives, and untimely Deaths.

To these mournful Narratives, I am about to add the Life of *Richard Savage*, a Man whose Writings entitle him to an eminent Rank in the Classes of Learning, and whose Misfortunes claim a Degree of Compassion, not always due to the unhappy, as they were often the Consequences of the Crimes of others, rather than his own.

In the Year 1697, *Anne* Countess of *Macclesfield*, having lived for some Time upon very uneasy Terms with her Husband, thought a public Confession of Adultery the most obvious and expeditious Method of obtaining her Liberty, and therefore declared, that the Child, with which she was then great, was begotten by the Earl *Rivers*. Her Husband, being as may be easily imagined, thus made no less desirous of a Separation than herself, prosecuted his Design in the most effectual Manner; for he applied not to the Ecclesiastical Courts for a Divorce, but to the Parliament for an Act, by which his Marriage might be dissolved, the nuptial Contract totally annulled, and the Child of his Wife illegitimated.[1] This Act, after the usual Deliberation, he obtained,

---

[1] Lady Macclesfield did not make a confession of adultery, but protested her innocence and did everything she could to conceal her affair with the Earl Rivers, defending herself in her husband's actions for divorce in both the Court of Arches and the House of Lords. Cf. Boswell, *Life*, i. 171. Johnson was led into this error by the anonymous *Life of Savage* (1727). Johnson ought to have learned the truth from both Thomas Salmon's *Review of the History of England* (1722–4) and the Journals of the House of Lords. (Though the Journals had not yet been printed, manuscript copies were easily available, and the entries concerning the Macclesfield case had been published in Ebenezer Timberland's *History and Proceedings of the House of Lords* (1742), ii. 2–3.)

Johnson, moreover, did not know that Lady Macclesfield had had a

tho' without the Approbation of some, who considered Marriage as an Affair only cognizable by Ecclesiastical Judges*; and next year on *March* 3d was separated from his Wife, whose Fortune, which was very great, was repaid her; and who having, as well as her Husband, the Liberty of making another Choice, was in a short Time married to Colonel *Bret*.

While the Earl of *Macclesfield* was prosecuting this Affair, his Wife was, on the tenth of *January* 1697–8,[2] delivered of a Son, and the Earl *Rivers*, by appearing to consider him as his own, left none any Reason to doubt of the Sincerity of her Declaration; for he was his Godfather, and gave him his own Name, which was by his Direction inserted in the Register of *St. Andrew*'s Parish in *Holbourn*,[3] but unfortunately left him to the Care of his Mother, whom,

---

* This Year was made remarkable by the Dissolution of a Marriage solemnised in the Face of the Church. *Salmon's Review.*

The following Protest is registered in the Books of the House of Lords.
  Dissentient.

Because we conceive that this is the first Bill of that Nature that hath passed, where there was not a Divorce first obtained in the Spiritual Court; which we look upon as an ill Precedent, and may be of dangerous Consequence in the future.
  Halifax.   Rochester.

---

previous child by Lord Rivers, a girl born in 1695. In writing this paragraph, following the language of the act of divorce, he had said 'the Children of his Wife', but in the second edition he altered 'Children' to 'Child'.

[2] The Countess's second child, the son that Savage said he was, was born on or about 16 Jan. 1697 (N.S.), not 10 Jan. 1698 (N.S.) (*The Manuscripts of the House of Lords, 1697–1699* (1905), pp. xxv, 57–67). The anonymous *Life* was again the source of Johnson's error; cf. p. 121 and n., and *AB*, p. 19.

[3] Earl Rivers stood godfather for his son, but under an assumed name, Captain John Smith, rather than his own, Richard Savage, so that the baptism was recorded under the name of Richard Smith. Unknown to Johnson, Savage had himself corrected the anonymous *Life* on this point, which was again the source of his error, in a letter to Mrs. Elizabeth Carter, saying that he had passed 'under another name' until the age of seventeen. (Montagu Pennington, *Memoirs of the Life of Mrs. Elizabeth Carter* (2nd edn., 1808), i. 58–61; Boswell, *Life*, i. 171 n.; *The Percy Letters*, i (1944), 208; cf. *AB*, p. 11.)

as she was now set free from her Husband, he probably imagined likely to treat with great Tenderness the Child that had contributed to so pleasing an Event. It is not indeed easy to discover what Motives could be found to over-balance that natural Affection of a Parent, or what Interest could be promoted by Neglect or Cruelty. The Dread of Shame or of Poverty, by which some Wretches have been incited to abandon or to murder their Children, cannot be supposed to have affected a Woman who had proclaimed her Crimes and solicited Reproach, and on whom the Clemency of the Legislature had undeservedly bestowed a Fortune, that would have been very little diminished by the Expences which the Care of her Child could have brought upon her. It was therefore not likely that she would be wicked without Temptation, that she would look upon her Son from his Birth with a kind of Resentment and Abhorrence; and instead of supporting, assisting, and de-fending him, delight to see him struggling with Misery; that she would take every Opportunity of aggravating his Misfortunes, and obstructing his Resources, and with an implacable and restless Cruelty continue her Persecution from the first Hour of his Life to the last.

But whatever were her Motives, no sooner was her Son born, than she discovered a Resolution of disowning him; and in a very short Time removed him from her Sight, by committing him to the Care of a poor Woman, whom she directed to educate him as her own, and injoined never to inform him of his true Parents.

Such was the Beginning of the Life of *Richard Savage*: Born with a legal Claim to Honour and to Riches, he was in two Months illegitimated by the Parliament, and dis-owned by his Mother, doomed to Poverty and Obscurity, and launched upon the Ocean of Life, only that he might be swallowed by its Quicksands, or dashed upon its Rocks.

His Mother could not indeed infect others with the same

Cruelty. As it was impossible to avoid the Inquiries which the Curiosity or Tenderness of her Relations made after her Child, she was obliged to give some Account of the Measures that she had taken, and her Mother, the Lady *Mason*, whether in Approbation of her Design, or to prevent more criminal Contrivances, engaged to transact with his Nurse, pay her for her Care, and superintend his Education.

In this charitable Office she was assisted by his Godmother Mrs. *Loyd*, who while she lived always looked upon him with that Tenderness, which the Barbarity of his Mother made peculiarly necessary; but her Death, which happened in his tenth Year, was another of the Misfortunes of his Childhood; for though she kindly endeavoured to alleviate his Loss by a Legacy of three hundred Pounds, yet as he had none to prosecute his Claim, or call in Law to the Assistance of Justice, her Will was eluded by the Executors, and no Part of the Money was ever paid.[4]

He was however not yet wholly abandoned. The Lady *Mason* still continued her Care, and directed him to be placed at a small Grammar School near St. *Alban*'s, where he was called by the Name of his Nurse, without the least Intimation that he had a Claim to any other.[5]

[4] Johnson followed the anonymous *Life* in believing that Savage had been taken care of first by 'a poor Woman' and afterwards by a Mrs. Lloyd, his godmother, who was well enough off to leave him a legacy of £300. But in his letter to Mrs. Carter, Savage had denied the existence of the first: 'As for . . . the mean nurse, she is quite a fictitious character. The person who took care of me, and as tenderly as the *apple of her eye*, (this expression is in a letter of her's, a copy of which I found many years after her decease among her papers) was one Mrs. Lloyd, a lady that kept her chariot, and lived accordingly.' The version of this story contained in *The Poetical Register* (1719–20) by Giles Jacob is closer to Savage's than the one in the anonymous *Life*, but it agrees in calling Mrs. Lloyd Savage's godmother. Savage himself never did so in any statement from him that has survived. The godmother of Richard Smith was Dorothy Ousley, wife of Lord Rivers's agent, of whom, however, Savage made no mention. Cf. *Notes and Queries*, 2nd Ser. vi (1858), 385–9.

[5] '. . . my Lady Mason, whether at her daughter's desire, or prompted by her own natural compassion, I shall not pretend to determine, transacted

Here he was initiated in Literature, and passed through several of the Classes, with what Rapidity or what Applause cannot now be known. As he always spoke with Respect of his Master, it is probable that the mean Rank, in which he then appeared, did not hinder his Genius from being distinguished, or his Industry from being rewarded, and if in so low a State he obtained Distinction and Rewards, it is not likely that they were gained but by Genius and Industry.

There is reason to conjecture, that his Application was equal to his Abilities, because his Improvement was more than proportioned to the Opportunities which he enjoyed; nor can it be doubted, that if his early Productions had been preserved, like those of happier Students, we might in some have found Sallies of that sprightly Humour, which distinguishes the *Author to be let*, and in others, Touches of that vigorous Imagination which painted the solemn Scenes of *the Wanderer*.

While he was thus cultivating his Mind, his Father the Earl *Rivers* was seized with a Distemper, which in a short Time put an End to his Life. He had frequently inquired after his Son, and had always been amused with fallacious and evasive Answers; but being now in his own Opinion on his Death-bed, he thought it his Duty to provide for him among his other natural Children, and therefore demanded a positive Account of him, with an Importunity not to be diverted or denied. His Mother, who could no longer refuse an Answer, determined at least to give such as should cut him off for ever from that Happiness which Com-

every thing with the nurse . . .' (Anonymous *Life*, p. 6). *The Poetical Register* stated that 'to his own Mother he has not been the least oblig'd for his education, but to her mother the Lady Mason'. The anonymous *Life* also said that he was sent 'to a little grammar school at St. Albans in Hertfordshire', but without naming his benefactress. Johnson had more information about Savage's schooling than came from either of these sources, to judge by the two paragraphs that follow. He must have questioned Savage.

petence affords, and therefore declared that he was dead; which is perhaps the first Instance of a Lie invented by a Mother to deprive her Son of a Provision which was designed him by another, and which she could not expect herself, though he should lose it.

This was therefore an Act of Wickedness which could not be defeated, because it could not be suspected; the Earl did not imagine, that there could exist in a human Form a Mother that would ruin her Son without enriching herself, and therefore bestowed upon some other Person six thousand Pounds, which he had in his Will bequeathed to *Savage*.[6]

The same Cruelty which incited his Mother to intercept this Provision which had been intended him, prompted her in a short Time to another Project, to a Project worthy of such a Disposition. She endeavoured to rid herself from the Danger of being at any Time made known to him, by sending him secretly to the *American* Plantations*.[7]

By whose Kindness this Scheme was counteracted, or by what Interposition she was induced to lay aside her Design, I know not; it is not improbable that the Lady *Mason* might persuade or compel her to desist, or perhaps she could not easily find Accomplices wicked enough to concur in so

---

* *Savage*'s Preface to his Miscellany.

[6] Lord Rivers died in 1712. The charge that he had been deceived as to his son's survival was made in all the early sources: *Poetical Register* (1719), *Plain Dealer*, No. 28 (1724), Preface to *Miscellaneous Poems* (1726), and the anonymous *Life* (1727). His will, made in 1711, contained several legacies to illegitimate children, and he added two codicils in June and July 1712, just before his death, in which he increased the number of such benefactions. So it is reasonable to believe that he would have left his son something had he known him to be still alive. Cf. *AB*, pp. 155–6.

[7] No date was given in any of the sources for the planned kidnapping. The anonymous *Life* mentioned it before the school at St. Albans and Lord Rivers's death. But in his Preface to *Miscellaneous Poems* Savage placed the episode immediately before another one that occurred when he was fifteen. Since Johnson believed Savage to have been born in 1698 and therefore to have been fifteen in 1713, he must have put the kidnapping after the death of Lord Rivers. Here he accepted the time-scheme of the Preface rather than that of the anonymous *Life*.

cruel an Action; for it may be conceived, that even those who had by a long Gradation of Guilt hardened their Hearts against the Sense of common Wickedness, would yet be shocked at the Design of a Mother to expose[8] her Son to Slavery and Want, to expose him without Interest, and without Provocation; and *Savage* might on this Occasion find Protectors and Advocates among those who had long traded in Crimes, and whom Compassion had never touched before.

Being hindered, by whatever Means, from banishing him into another Country, she formed soon after a Scheme for burying him in Poverty and Obscurity in his own; and that his Station of Life, if not the Place of his Residence, might keep him for ever at a Distance from her, she ordered him to be placed with a Shoemaker in *Holbourn*, that after the usual Time of Trial, he might become his Apprentice*.

It is generally reported, that this Project was for some time successful, and that *Savage* was employed at the Awl longer than he was willing to confess; nor was it perhaps any great Advantage to him, that an unexpected Discovery determined him to quit his Occupation.[9]

About this Time his Nurse, who had always treated him as her own Son, died; and it was natural for him to take

---

* Preface to *Savage*'s Miscellanies.

---

[8] This word was often used by Johnson with reference to Lady Macclesfield's treatment of Savage, suggesting the ancient practice of infanticide by exposure; cf. pp. 20, 75, 109. In his Preface to *Miscellaneous Poems* Savage quoted several passages from Locke bearing on this and other barbarous practices, adding: 'Were I inclinable to grow serious, I could easily prove that I have not been more gently dealt with by Mrs. *Bret*.' Cf. p. 28 n. Johnson quoted one of these passages from Locke in his *Dictionary* s.v. 'expose'. By 1768 he had apparently come to think that he had been too hard on Savage's supposed mother. Cf. *Boswell in Search of a Wife*, ed. Frank Brady and Frederick A. Pottle (New York, 1956), p. 168.

[9] In his Preface to *Miscellaneous Poems* Savage wrote that this episode occurred when he was fifteen and that he declined to become a shoemaker. Johnson, who had perhaps made inquiries among Savage's acquaintances, contradicted him as to the refusal and added a fact not mentioned elsewhere, that the master shoemaker lived in Holborn.

Care of those Effects which by her Death were, as he imagined, become his own; he therefore went to her House, opened her Boxes, and examined her Papers, among which he found some Letters written to her by the Lady *Mason*, which informed him of his Birth, and the Reasons for which it was concealed.[10]

He was now no longer satisfied with the Employment which had been allotted him, but thought he had a Right to share the Affluence of his Mother, and therefore without Scruple applied to her as her Son, and made use of every Art to awaken her Tenderness, and attract her Regard. But neither his Letters, nor the Interposition of those Friends which his Merit or his Distress procured him, made any Impression upon her: She still resolved to neglect, though she could no longer disown him.

It was to no Purpose that he frequently solicited her to admit him to see her; she avoided him with the most vigilant Precaution, and ordered him to be excluded from her

---

[10] Johnson evidently believed that the nurse who died leaving the letters Savage discovered was the poor woman mentioned earlier, not Mrs. Lloyd. He accepted the statement of the anonymous *Life* that their discovery had been made when Savage was about fifteen. They had allegedly been addressed to the nurse by Lady Mason. But if the poor woman never existed and Savage had been taken care of by Mrs. Lloyd, the letters must have been found among her effects. He spoke of his having also a letter written by her. But she died when he was seven (*Poetical Register* said ten), much too young to take the action Johnson described. Nevertheless, since the facts of the divorce had been successfully hushed up at the time, Savage must have put his hands on something to give him the information he made use of.

These letters, whatever they were, most likely made up the file of 'convincing *Original Letters*' that he sent to Aaron Hill in 1724 with a covering letter stating that they had been put together in order to be shown to 'a Hand [*sic*], too *Just*, and too *Powerful*, to leave me the least Distrust of being, shortly, *less oppressed than I have been*'. Hill printed part of this letter in the *Plain Dealer*, no. 73 (30 Nov. 1724), saying that 'the Proofs he sent me, are too *strong*, to be easily mistaken'. Who the just and powerful 'Hand' was is a matter for conjecture, Lord Tyrconnel being the likeliest guess. Shortly afterwards he did take Savage into his protection, and at the same time he may have also got these letters into his power, feeling safer with them no longer in Savage's hands, even though his attitude towards his aunt, Mrs. Brett, was not sympathetic.

House, by whomsoever he might be introduced, and what Reason soever he might give for entering it.

Savage was at the same Time so touched with the Discovery of his real Mother, that it was his frequent Practice to walk in the dark Evenings* for several Hours before her Door, in Hopes of seeing her as she might come by Accident to the Window, or cross her Apartment with a Candle in her Hand.[11]

But all his Assiduity and Tenderness were without Effect, for he could neither soften her Heart, nor open her Hand, and was reduced to the utmost Miseries of Want, while he was endeavouring to awaken the Affection of a Mother: He was therefore obliged to seek some other Means of Support, and having no Profession, became, by Necessity, an Author.

At this Time the Attention of all the literary World was engrossed by the *Bangorian* Controversy, which filled the Press with Pamphlets, and the Coffee-houses with Disputants. Of this Subject, as most popular, he made Choice for his first Attempt, and without any other Knowledge of the Question, than he had casually collected from Conversation, published a Poem against the Bishop.

What was the Success or Merit of this Performance I know not, it was probably lost among the innumerable Pamphlets to which that Dispute gave Occasion. Mr. *Savage* was himself in a little time ashamed of it, and endeavoured to suppress it, by destroying all the Copies that he could collect.[12]

* *Plain Dealer.*

---

[11] This anecdote came from a letter in *Plain Dealer*, no. 28 (26 June 1724), written by 'Amintas', most likely an alias of Aaron Hill's.

[12] The Bangorian Controversy was an aftermath of the Jacobite rising of 1715. In 1717 the Lower House of Convocation, which was predominantly High Church, condemned Benjamin Hoadly, the whig Bishop of Bangor, on account of two of his sermons, with the result that the Government prorogued Convocation and never again allowed it to transact synodical business. This arbitrary action was followed by a furious

He then attempted a more gainful Kind of Writing*, and in his eighteenth Year offered to the Stage a Comedy borrowed from a *Spanish* Plot, which was refused by the Players, and was therefore given by him to Mr. *Bullock*, who having more Interest, made some slight Alterations, and brought it upon the Stage, under the Title of †*Woman's a Riddle*, but allowed the unhappy Author no Part of the Profit.[13]

Not discouraged however at this Repulse, he wrote two Years afterwards *Love in a Veil*, another Comedy, borrowed likewise from the *Spanish*, but with little better Success than before; for though it was received and acted, yet it appeared so late in the Year, that the Author obtained no other Advantage from it, than the Acquaintance of Sir *Richard Steele*, and Mr. *Wilks*; by whom he was pitied, caressed, and relieved.[14]

Sir *Richard Steele* having declared in his Favour with all the Ardour of Benevolence which constituted his Character, promoted his Interest with the utmost Zeal, related his Misfortunes, applauded his Merit, took all Opportunities of recommending him, and asserted‡ that *the Inhumanity of his Mother had given him a Right to find every good Man his Father.*[15]

* *Jacob's* Lives of Dramatic Poets.
† This Play was printed first in 8vo, and afterwards in 12mo, the fifth Edition.
‡ *Plain Dealer.*

---

controversy carried on in the pulpits, the newspapers, and the theatres. In the *Convocation*, written in the summer or fall of 1717 and published later the same year, Savage gave an account of the controversy from a High Church point of view.

[13] Johnson's account of this play derived mainly from the anonymous *Life*. It was produced in 1716, and does not appear to be Savage's work. Cf. *AB*, pp. 38–41.

[14] *Love in a Veil* was produced at Drury Lane on 17 June 1718 and published later the same year. The absence of critical comment suggests that Johnson had not read it, all the facts he gave being available in the anonymous *Life*.

[15] 'I think it was finely said, by a Gentleman, whose Writings, and

Nor was Mr. *Savage* admitted to his Acquaintance only, but to his Confidence, of which he sometimes related an Instance too extraordinary to be omitted, as it affords a very just Idea of his Patron's Character.

He was once desired by Sir *Richard*, with an Air of the utmost Importance, to come very early to his House the next Morning. Mr. *Savage* came as he had promised, found the Chariot at the Door, and Sir *Richard* waiting for him, and ready to go out. What was intended, and whither they were to go, *Savage* could not conjecture, and was not willing to enquire; but immediately seated himself with his Friend; the Coachman was ordered to drive, and they hurried with the utmost Expedition to *Hyde-park Corner*, where they stopped at a petty Tavern, and retired to a private Room. Sir *Richard* then informed him, that he intended to publish a Pamphlet, and that he had desired him to come thither that he might write for him. They soon sat down to the Work, Sir *Richard* dictated, and *Savage* wrote, till the Dinner that had been ordered was put upon the Table. *Savage* was surprised at the Meanness of the Entertainment, and after some Hesitation, ventured to ask for Wine, which Sir *Richard*, not without Reluctance, ordered to be brought. They then finished their Dinner, and proceeded in their Pamphlet, which they concluded in the Afternoon.

Mr. *Savage* then imagined his Task over, and expected that Sir *Richard* would call for the Reckoning, and return home; but his Expectations deceived him, for Sir *Richard* told him, that he was without Money, and that the Pamphlet must be sold before the Dinner could be paid for; and

Humanity, were, for many Years, the Admiration of the Kingdom—*That it ought to be the Care of All, in whose Power it lay, to lift Mr.* SAVAGE *above a Sense of his* MOTHER's *Cruelty; because a Misery, so undeserved, had intitled him to a Right of finding Every Good Man his* FATHER.' (*Plain Dealer*, no. 73 (30 Nov. 1724.)) A reason for the withholding of Steele's name is suggested on p. 16 and n.; cf. pp. 47 and n., and 110 and n.

Savage was therefore obliged to go and offer their new Production to Sale for two Guineas, which with some Difficulty he obtained. Sir *Richard* then returned home, having retired that Day only to avoid his Creditors, and composed the Pamphlet only to discharge his Reckoning.

Mr. *Savage* related another Fact equally uncommon, which, though it has no Relation to his Life, ought to be preserved. Sir *Richard Steele* having one Day invited to his House a great Number of Persons of the first Quality, they were surprised at the Number of Liveries which surrounded the Table; and after Dinner, when Wine and Mirth had set them free from the Observation of rigid Ceremony, one of them enquired of Sir *Richard*, how such an expensive Train of Domestics could be consistent with his Fortune. He with great Frankness confessed, that they were Fellows of whom he would very willingly be rid. And being then asked, why he did not discharge them, declared that they were Bailiffs who had introduced themselves with an Execution, and whom, since he could not send them away, he had thought it convenient to embellish with Liveries, that they might do him Credit while they staid.

His Friends were diverted with the Expedient, and by paying the Debt discharged their Attendance, having obliged Sir *Richard* to promise that they should never again find him graced with a Retinue of the same Kind.

Under such a Tutor, Mr. *Savage* was not likely to learn Prudence or Frugality, and perhaps many of the Misfortunes which the Want of those Virtues brought upon him in the following Parts of his Life, might be justly imputed to so unimproving an Example.

Nor did the Kindness of Sir *Richard* end in common Favours. He proposed to have established him in some settled Scheme of Life, and to have contracted a Kind of Alliance with him, by marrying him to a natural Daughter, on whom he intended to bestow a thousand Pounds. But though he was always lavish of future Bounties, he conducted his Affairs in such a Manner, that he was very seldom able to keep his Promises, or execute his own Intentions; and as he was never able to raise the Sum which he had offered, the Marriage was delayed. In the mean time he was officiously informed that Mr. *Savage* had ridiculed him; by which he was so much exasperated, that he withdrew the Allowance which he had paid him, and never afterwards admitted him to his House.

It is not indeed unlikely that *Savage* might by his Imprudence expose himself to the Malice of a Tale-bearer; for his Patron had many Follies, which as his Discernment easily discovered, his Imagination might sometimes incite him to mention too ludicrously. A little Knowledge of the World is sufficient to discover that such Weakness is very common, and that there are few who do not sometimes in the Wantonness of thoughtless Mirth, or the Heat of transient Resentment, speak of their Friends and Benefactors with Levity and Contempt, though in their cooler Moments, they want neither Sense of their Kindness, nor Reverence for their Virtue. The Fault therefore of Mr. *Savage* was rather Negligence than Ingratitude; but Sir *Richard* must likewise be acquitted of Severity, for who is there that can patiently bear Contempt from one whom he has relieved and supported, whose Establishment he has laboured, and whose Interest he has promoted?[16]

[16] The anonymous *Life,* though giving some of the information used here, did not mention Sir Richard Steele by name, but called him 'a certain Knight, whose Name is not a little known by his Writings'. Savage must have frequently told Johnson stories about Steele, enabling him to identify the 'certain Knight' and introduce two amusing but irrelevant anecdotes about his debts. As late as 1779–81 he remembered another, and introduced it into his life of Addison. His information about the proposal to marry Savage to Steele's natural daughter, however, came entirely from the anonymous *Life*; for Savage gave Mrs. Carter a different version: 'The certain knight . . . was Sir Richard Steele; but that account of what passed between me and him is partly true, and partly not so. That there was a slander raised against me, which caused a difference

He was now again abandoned to Fortune, without any other Friend than Mr. *Wilks*; a Man, who, whatever were his Abilities or Skill as an Actor, deserves at least to be remembered for his Virtues*, which are not often to be found in the World, and perhaps less often in his Profession than in others. To be humane, generous and candid, is a very high Degree of Merit in any State; but those Qualities deserve still greater Praise, when they are found in that Condition, which makes almost every other Man, for whatever Reason, contemptuous, insolent, petulant, selfish, and brutal.

* As it is a Loss to Mankind, when any good Action is forgotten, I shall insert another Instance of Mr. *Wilks*'s Generosity, very little known. Mr. *Smith*, a Gentleman educated at *Dublin*, being hindred by an Impediment in his Pronunciation from engaging in Orders, for which his Friends designed him, left his own Country, and came to *London* in Quest of Employment, but found his Solicitations fruitless, and his Necessities every Day more pressing. In this Distress he wrote a Tragedy, and offered it to the Players, by whom it was rejected. Thus were his last Hopes defeated, and he had no other Prospect than of the most deplorable Poverty. But Mr. *Wilks* thought his Performance, though not perfect, at least worthy of some Reward, and therefore offered him a Benefit. This Favour he improved with so much Diligence, that the House afforded him a considerable Sum, with which he went to *Leyden*, applied himself to the Study of Physic, and prosecuted his Design with so much Diligence and Success, that when Dr. *Boerhaave* was desired by the Czarina to recommend proper Persons to introduce into *Russia* the Practice and Study of Physic, Dr. *Smith* was one of those whom he selected. He had a considerable Pension settled on him at his Arrival, and was one of the chief Physicians at the *Russian* Court.

between us, which lasted a long while, is truth, and the worthy Mr. Curll, the bookseller, was the person who raised it; but we were afterwards reconciled, he being fully convinced of my innocence. As for the constant allowance I received from him, the author is quite mistaken; I never had any such, not even a single present from Sir Richard Steele; and how can he be said to have withheld a bounty which he never bestowed? As to the proposal of my marrying his natural daughter, the reasons why, and the terms on which he proposed it, the author has not erred in; but as to the reason why the match did not go on, he is again mistaken. The truth is this: I quite declined the proposal, and never could be induced to see the lady, though he frequently and warmly pressed me to an interview, nor have I to this day ever seen her.' (*Memoirs of Mrs. Carter*, pp. 59–60.) The reconciliation, however, does not seem to have occurred—a fact that may explain the unwillingness of both the *Plain Dealer* and the anonymous *Life* to use Steele's name in connection with Savage's.

As Mr. *Wilks* was one of those to whom Calamity seldom complained without Relief, he naturally took an unfortunate Wit into his Protection, and not only assisted him in any casual Distresses, but continued an equal and steady Kindness to the Time of his Death.

By his Interposition Mr. *Savage* once obtained from his Mother* fifty Pounds, and a Promise of one hundred and fifty more; but it was the Fate of this unhappy Man, that few Promises of any Advantage to him were performed. His Mother was infected among others with the general Madness of the *South-Sea* Traffick, and having been disappointed in her Expectations, refused to pay what perhaps nothing but the Prospect of sudden Affluence prompted her to promise.

Being thus obliged to depend upon the Friendship of Mr. *Wilks*, he was consequently an assiduous Frequenter of the Theatres, and in a short Time the Amusements of the Stage took such Possession of his Mind, that he never was absent from a Play in several Years.[17]

This constant Attendance naturally procured him the Acquaintance of the Players, and among others, of Mrs. *Oldfield*, who was so much pleased with his Conversation,

* This I write upon the Credit of the Author of his Life, which was published 1727.

[17] Savage told Mrs. Carter that he had received no financial aid from Wilks, but he may have referred to a regular pension rather than to the help in 'casual Distresses' mentioned by Johnson. Wilks gave him benefit performances at Drury Lane twice: 2 Oct. 1723 and 17 Feb. 1731.

Johnson's careful citation of the anonymous *Life* as his authority for the further statement that Wilks also got money for Savage from Mrs. Brett may betray scepticism. It had not actually named Mrs. Brett, but described the source of the money as 'a Lady, whose Duty it seem'd to have been to take some Care of him'. Cf. Eliza Haywood's *Memoirs of a Certain Island Adjacent to the Kingdom of Utopia* (2nd edn., 1726), i. 187, and Daniel O'Bryan's *Authentic Memoirs . . . of . . . Mr. Robert Wilks* (1732), pp. 25–6.

The anecdote about Mr. Smith may have come to Johnson by word of mouth, perhaps Savage's, and was repeated in W. R. Chetwood's *General History of the Stage* (1749), pp. 239–42, where a letter is also printed written by Smith in St. Petersburgh.

and touched with his Misfortunes, that she allowed him a settled Pension of fifty Pounds a Year, which was during her Life regularly paid.

That this Act of Generosity may receive it's due Praise, and that the good Actions of Mrs. *Oldfield* may not be sullied by her general Character, it is proper to mention what Mr. *Savage* often declared in the strongest Terms, that he never saw her alone, or in any other Place than behind the Scenes.

At her Death, he endeavoured to shew his Gratitude in the most decent Manner, by wearing Mourning as for a Mother, but did not celebrate her in Elegies, because he knew that too great Profusion of Praise would only have revived those Faults which his natural Equity did not allow him to think less, because they were committed by one who favoured him; but of which, though his Virtue would not endeavour to palliate them, his Gratitude would not suffer him to prolong the Memory, or diffuse the Censure.

In his *Wanderer*, he has indeed taken an Opportunity of mentioning her, but celebrates her not for her Virtue, but her Beauty, an Excellence which none ever denied her: This is the only Encomium with which he has rewarded her Liberality, and perhaps he has even in this been too lavish of his Praise. He seems to have thought that never to mention his Benefactress, would have an Appearance of Ingratitude, though to have dedicated any particular Performance to her Memory, would have only betrayed an officious Partiality, that without exalting her Character, would have depressed his own.[18]

He had sometimes, by the Kindness of Mr. *Wilks*, the Advantage of a Benefit, on which Occasions he often received uncommon Marks of Regard and Compassion; and

[18] Johnson's information about Savage's relations with Mrs. Oldfield must have come mainly from Savage himself, since she is not mentioned in the anonymous *Life* or any of the other printed sources. Cf. *AB*, pp. 45–8.

was once told by the Duke of *Dorset*, that it was just to consider him as an injured Nobleman, and that in his Opinion the Nobility ought to think themselves obliged without Solicitation to take every Opportunity of supporting him by their Countenance and Patronage. But he had generally the Mortification to hear that the whole Interest of his Mother was employed to frustrate his Applications, and that she never left any Expedient untried, by which he might be cut off from the Possibility of supporting Life. The same Disposition she endeavoured to diffuse among all those over whom Nature or Fortune gave her any Influence, and indeed succeeded too well in her Design; but could not always propagate her Effrontery with her Cruelty, for some of those whom she incited against him, were ashamed of their own Conduct, and boasted of that Relief which they never gave him.

In this Censure I do not indiscriminately involve all his Relations; for he has mentioned with Gratitude the Humanity of one Lady, whose Name I am now unable to recollect, and to whom therefore I cannot pay the Praises which she deserves for having acted well in Opposition to Influence, Precept, and Example.

The Punishment which our Laws inflict upon those Parents who murder their Infants, is well known, nor has its Justice ever been contested; but if they deserve Death who destroy a Child in it's Birth, what Pains can be severe enough for her who forbears to destroy him only to inflict sharper Miseries upon him; who prolongs his Life only to make it miserable; and who exposes him without Care and without Pity, to the Malice of Oppression, the Caprices of Chance, and the Temptations of Poverty; who rejoices to see him overwhelmed with Calamities; and when his own Industry, or the Charity of others, has enabled him to rise for a short Time above his Miseries, plunges him again into his former Distress?

The Kindness of his Friends not affording him any constant Supply, and the Prospect of improving his Fortune, by enlarging his Acquaintance, necessarily leading him to Places of Expence, he found it necessary* to endeavour once more at dramatic Poetry, for which he was now better qualified by a more extensive Knowledge, and longer Observation. But having been unsuccessful in Comedy, though rather for Want of Opportunities than Genius, he resolved now to try whether he should not be more fortunate in exhibiting a Tragedy.

The Story which he chose for the Subject, was that of Sir *Thomas Overbury*, a Story well adapted to the Stage, though perhaps not far enough removed from the present Age, to admit properly the Fictions necessary to complete the Plan; for the Mind which naturally loves Truth is always most offended with the Violation of those Truths of which we are most certain, and we of course conceive those Facts most certain which approach nearest to our own Time.

Out of this Story he formed a Tragedy, which, if the Circumstances in which he wrote it be considered, will afford at once an uncommon Proof of Strength of Genius, and Evenness of Mind, of a Serenity not to be ruffled, and an Imagination not to be suppressed.

During a considerable Part of the Time, in which he was employed upon this Performance, he was without Lodging, and often without Meat; nor had he any other Conveniences for Study than the Fields or the Streets allowed him, there he used to walk and form his Speeches, and afterwards step into a Shop, beg for a few Moments the Use of the Pen and Ink, and write down what he had composed upon Paper which he had picked up by Accident.

If the Performance of a Writer thus distressed is not perfect, its Faults ought surely to be imputed to a Cause very

* In 1724.

different from Want of Genius, and must rather excite Pity than provoke Censure.[19]

But when under these Discouragements the Tragedy was finished, there yet remained the Labour of introducing it on the Stage, an Undertaking which to an ingenuous Mind was in a very high Degree vexatious and disgusting; for having little Interest or Reputation, he was obliged to submit himself wholly to the Players, and admit, with whatever Reluctance, the Emendations of Mr. *Cibber*, which he always considered as the Disgrace of his Performance.[20]

He had indeed in Mr. *Hill* another Critic of a very different Class, from whose Friendship he received great Assistance on many Occasions, and whom he never mentioned but with the utmost Tenderness and Regard*. He

---

* He inscribed to him a short Poem, called *The Friend*, printed in his Miscellanies, in which he addresses him with the utmost Ardour of Affection

> O lov'd *Hillarius*! thou by Heav'n design'd
> To charm, to mend, and to instruct Mankind:
> To whom my Hopes, Fears, Joys, and Sorrows tend,
> Thou Brother, Father, nearer yet—thou Friend——
> —Kind are my Wrongs, I thence thy Friendship own,
> What State could bless, were I to thee unknown?
> ——While shun'd, obscur'd, or thwarted and expos'd,
> By Friends abandon'd, and by Foes enclos'd,
> Thy Guardian Counsel softens ev'ry Care,
> To Ease sooths Anguish, and to Hope, Despair.

---

[19] For what he wrote about *Sir Thomas Overbury* Johnson was not much indebted to the anonymous *Life*, which dismissed it quickly. Savage must have been his informant. The play was written in 1723, produced on 12 June, and published the following year. Johnson evidently considered it important and worth the exercise of his critical powers. It must be almost the earliest work by Savage that he had read.

[20] Since the printed sources made no references to the difficulties mentioned in this paragraph, Johnson must have got this information from Savage. By 'Mr.' Cibber he seems to have meant Colley Cibber, the actor and dramatist, who, as manager of Drury Lane, might have insisted on alterations. But Johnson's use of the prefix 'Mr.' is erratic, and it was the younger Cibber, Theophilus, from whom Savage himself in his Dedication acknowledged help—an acknowledgement he later regretted. Cf. p. 24 Johnson originally alluded to 'the Mists which Poverty and *Cibber* had been able to spread over' this play, but in the second edition he cut out 'and *Cibber*'.

had been for some Time distinguished by him with very particular Kindness, and on this Occasion it was natural to apply to him as an Author of an established Character. He therefore sent this Tragedy to him with a short Copy of Verses*, in which he desired his Correction. Mr. *Hill*, whose Humanity and Politeness are generally known, readily complied with his Request; but as he is remarkable for singularity of Sentiment, and bold Experiments in Language, Mr. *Savage* did not think his Play much improved by his Innovation, and had even at that Time the Courage to reject several Passages which he could not approve, and what is still more laudable, Mr. *Hill* had the Generosity not to resent the Neglect of his Alterations, but wrote the Prologue and Epilogue, in which he touches on the Circumstances of the Author with great Tenderness†.[21]

---

* *To* A. HILL, Esq; *with the Tragedy of Sir*
THOMAS OVERBURY.

As the Soul strip'd of mortal Clay
  Shews all divinely fair,
And boundless roves the Milky Way,
  And views sweet Prospects there.
This Hero clog'd with drossy Lines
  By thee new Vigour tries;
As thy correcting Hand refines
  Bright Scenes around him rise.
Thy Touch brings the wish'd Stone to pass,
  So sought, so long foretold;
It turns polluted Lead and Brass
  At once to purest Gold.

† In a full World our Author lives alone,
  Unhappy, and by Consequence unknown;
  Yet amidst Sorrow he disdains Complaint,
  Nor languid in the Race of Life grows faint:
  He swims, unyielding, against Fortune's Stream,
  Nor to his private Sufferings stoops his Theme.

---

[21] Most of Johnson's facts came from the anonymous *Life*, but Savage himself must have told him that he had not thought highly of Hill's improvements. Johnson may have been correct in stating that Hill did not resent Savage's rejection of several of them, but in a letter to Benjamin

After all these Obstructions and Compliances, he was only able to bring his Play upon the Stage in the Summer, when the chief Actors had retired, and the rest were in Possession of the House for their own Advantage. Among these Mr. *Savage* was admitted to play the Part of Sir *Thomas Overbury*, by which he gained no great Reputation, the Theatre being a Province for which Nature seemed not to have designed him; for neither his Voice, Look, nor Gesture, were such as are expected on the Stage, and he was himself so much ashamed of having been reduced to appear as a Player, that he always blotted out his Name from the List, when a Copy of his Tragedy was to be shown to his Friends.

In the Publication of his Performance he was more successful, for the Rays of Genius that glimmered in it, that glimmered through all the Mists which Poverty had been able to spread over it, procured him the Notice and Esteem of many Persons eminent for their Rank, their Virtue, and their Wit.

Of this Play, acted, printed, and dedicated, the accumulated Profits arose to an hundred Pounds, which he thought at that Time a very large Sum, having been never Master of so much before.

In the Dedication*, for which he received ten Guineas, there is nothing remarkable. The Preface contains a very liberal Encomium on the blooming Excellencies of Mr. *Theophilus Cibber*, which Mr. *Savage* could not in the latter Part of his Life see his Friends about to read without snatching the Play out of their Hands.

The Generosity of Mr. *Hill* did not end on this Occasion;

* To *Herbert Tryst*, Esq; of *Herefordshire*.

Victor written in Feb. 1723, Hill confessed to being full of 'spleen and resentment' against Savage (Victor's *History of the Theatres of London and Dublin* (1761), ii. 171). The reference, however, may have been to a different incident (cf. *European Magazine*, vi (1784), 192-3, 279), because Hill wrote the Prologue for Savage's play and asked him for six tickets.

for afterwards when Mr. *Savage's* Necessities returned, he
encouraged a Subscription to a Miscellany of Poems in a
very extraordinary Manner, by publishing his Story in the
*Plain Dealer**, with some affecting Lines†, which he asserts
to have been written by Mr. *Savage* upon the Treatment
received by him from his Mother, but of which he was
himself the Author, as Mr. *Savage* afterwards declared.[22]

* The *Plain Dealer* was a periodical Paper written by Mr. *Hill* and Mr.
Bond, whom Mr. *Savage* called the two contending Powers of Light and
Darkness. They wrote by turns each six Essays, and the Character of the
Work was observed regularly to rise in Mr. *Hill's* Weeks, and fall in
Mr. *Bond's*.

> † Hopeless, abandoned, aimless, and oppress'd,
> Lost to Delight, and, ev'ry Way, distress'd;
> Cross his cold Bed, in wild Disorder, thrown,
> Thus sigh'd *Alexis*, friendless, and alone ——
> Why do I breathe?——What Joy can Being give?
> When she, who gave me Life, forgets I live!
> Feels not these wintry Blasts;——nor heeds my Smart;
> But shuts me from the Shelter of her Heart!
> Saw me expos'd to Want! to Shame! to Scorn!
> To Ills!——which make it *Misery*, to be *born*!
> Cast me, regardless, on the World's bleak Wild;
> And bade me be a Wretch, while yet a Child!
> Where can he hope for Pity, Peace, or Rest,
> Who moves no Softness in a Mother's Breast?
> Custom, Law, Reason, *all*! my Cause forsake,
> And *Nature sleeps*, to keep my Woes *awake*!
> Crimes, which the *Cruel* scarce believe can be,
> The *Kind* are guilty of, to ruin *me*.
> Ev'n she, who bore me, blasts me with her Hate,
> And, *meant* my *Fortune*, *makes* herself my *Fate*.
> Yet has this sweet Neglecter of my Woes,
> The softest, tend'rest Breast, that *Pity* knows!
> Her Eyes shed Mercy, wheresoe'er they shine;
> And her Soul *melts* at ev'ry Woe—but *mine*.
> Sure then! some secret Fate, for Guilt unwill'd,
> Some Sentence pre-ordain'd to be fulfill'd!
> Plung'd me, thus deep, in Sorrow's searching Flood;
> And wash'd me from the Mem'ry of her Blood.
> But, Oh! whatever Cause has mov'd her Hate,
> Let me but sigh, in Silence, at my Fate;
> The God, *within*, perhaps may touch her Breast;
> And, when she *pities*, who can be distress'd?

[22] The *Plain Dealer* first mentioned Savage in no. 15 (11 May 1724),

These Lines, and the Paper in which they were inserted, had a very powerful Effect upon all but his Mother, whom by making her Cruelty more publick, they only hardened in her Aversion.

Mr. *Hill* not only promoted the Subscription to the Miscellany, but furnished likewise the greatest Part of the Poems of which it is composed, and particularly *the Happy Man*, which he published as a Specimen.

The Subscriptions of those whom these Papers should influence to patronise Merit in Distress, without any other Solicitation, were directed to be left at *Button*'s Coffee-house, and Mr. *Savage* going thither a few Days afterwards, without Expectation of any Effect from his Proposal, found to his Surprise seventy Guineas*, which had been sent him in Consequence of the Compassion excited by Mr. *Hill*'s pathetic Representation.

* The Names of those who so generously contributed to his Relief, having been mentioned in a former Account, ought not to be omitted here. They were the Dutchess of *Cleveland*, Lady *Cheyney*, Lady *Castlemain*, Lady *Gower*, Lady *Lechmere*, the Dutchess Dowager, and Dutchess of *Rutland*, Lady *Strafford*, the Countess Dowager of *Warwick*, Mrs. *Mary Floyer*, Mrs. *Sofuel Noel*, Duke of *Rutland*, Lord *Gainsborough*, Lord *Milsington*, Mr. *John Savage*.[23]

publishing his lines 'To a Young Gentleman' with his name. It returned to him in no. 28 (26 June 1724) in a letter from 'Amintas' that gave a brief sketch of his life including the story of his walking by night under his mother's window, followed by Hill's 'affecting lines'. Cf. *Works of the Late Aaron Hill* (1753), iv. 51–3. Though Savage's name was not mentioned in this essay, there was a cross-reference to no. 15. A third essay was planned as early as 13 Aug. (cf. *European Magazine*, vi (1784), 194), but did not appear until 30 Nov. (no. 73). It contained a letter from Savage in which he referred to his file of original letters (cf. p. 11 and n.) and described the proposed miscellany of poems, giving the text of Hill's 'Happy Man' as a sample.

Evidently Johnson knew nothing of the first number of the *Plain Dealer*, and seems to have thought of the other two as one. At first he had thought of reprinting it in an appendix (cf. p. 12 and textual note).

[23] Johnson's list of names came from the anonymous *Life*, which had accidentally omitted one, that of William Baynton, Esq., rather than from its source, *Miscellaneous Poems*. Johnson rearranged the names so as to put ladies before gentlemen and persons having titles before ones without them.

To this Miscellany he publish'd a Preface*, in which he gives an Account of his Mother's Cruelty in a very uncommon Strain of Humour, and with a Gaiety of Imagination, which the Success of his Subscription probably produced.[24]

* This Preface is as follows:
Crudelis Mater magis, an Puer improbus ille?
Improbus ille Puer, crudelis tu quoque Mater. Virg.

My Readers, I am afraid, when they observe *Richard Savage* join'd so close, and so constantly, to *Son of the late Earl* Rivers, will impute to a ridiculous Vanity, what is the Effect of an unhappy Necessity, which my hard Fortune has thrown me under———I am to be pardoned for adhering a little tenaciously to my Father, because my Mother will allow me to be No-body; and has almost reduced me, among heavier Afflictions, to that uncommon Kind of Want, which the *Indians* of *America* complained of at our first settling among them; when they came to beg *Names* of the *English, because* (said they) *we are poor Men of ourselves, and have none we can lay Claim to.*

The good Nature of those, to whom I have not the Honour to be known, would forgive me the ludicrous Turn of this Beginning, if they knew but how little Reason I have to be merry———It was my Misfortune to be Son of the above-mentioned Earl, by the late Countess of *Macclesfield*, (now Widow of Colonel *Henry Bret;*) whose Divorce, on Occasion of the Amour which I was a Consequence of, has left something on Record, which I take to be very remarkable; and it is this: Certain of our great Judges, in their *temporal* Decisions, act with a *spiritual* Regard to the *Levitical Divinity*; and in particular to the Ten Commandments: Two of which seem in my Case, to have visibly influenced their Opinions———*Thou shalt not commit Adultery*, pointed fullest on my Mother: But, as to *The Lord's visiting the Sins of the Fathers on the Children*, it was considered as what could regard *me* only: And for that Reason, I suppose, it had been inconsistent with the Rules of Sanctity, to assign Provision out of my Mother's return'd Estate, for Support of an Infant Sinner.

Thus, while *legally* the Son of one Earl, and *naturally* of another, I am, *nominally*, No-body's Son at all: For the Lady, having given me *too much Father*, thought it but an equivalent Deduction, to leave me *no Mother*, by Way of Balance———So I came sported into the World, a Kind of Shuttlecock, between Law and Nature———If Law had not beaten me back, by the Stroke of an Act, on purpose, I had now been *above Wit*, by the Privilege of a Man of Quality: Nay, I might have preserved into the Bargain, the Lives of *Duke Hamilton* and *Lord Mohun*, whose Dispute arose from the Estate of that Earl of *Macclesfield*, whom (but for the mentioned Act) I must have *called Father*———And, if Nature had not struck me off, with a stranger Blow than Law did, the other Earl, who was

[24] Though Johnson did not think highly of this preface as a literary work, he accepted several of its statements as biographical evidence. Cf. *AB*, pp. 76-8, 94-5.

The Dedication is addressed to the Lady *Mary Wortley Montague*, whom he flatters without Reserve, and, to con-

most *emphatically* my Father, could never have been told, I was *dead*, when he was about to enable me, by his *Will*, to have *lived* to some Purpose. An unaccountable Severity of a *Mother*! whom I was then not old enough to have deserved it from: And by which I am a single unhappy Instance, among that Nobleman's natural Children; and thrown, friendless on the World, without Means of supporting *myself*; and without Authority to apply to those, whose Duty I know it is to support me.

Thus however ill qualified I am to *live by my Wits*, I have the best Plea in the World for attempting it; since it is too apparent, that I was *born to it*——Having wearied my Judgment with fruitless Endeavours to be *happy*, I gave the Reins to my Fancy, that I might learn, at least, to be *easy*.

But I cease awhile to speak of *myself*, that I may say something of my Miscellany——I was furnished, by the Verses of my Friends, with *Wit* enough to deserve a Subscription; but I wanted another much more profitable Quality, which should have emboldened me to solicite it: By means of which natural Defect, (another of my Wants, that, I *hope*, may be imputed to my Mother!) I had met with little Encouragement, but for the Endeavours of some few Gentlemen, in my Behalf, who were generous enough to consider my ill Fortune, as a Merit that intitled me to their Notice.

Among these I am particularly indebted to the Author of the *Plain Dealers*, who was pleased, in two of his Papers, (which I intreat his Pardon, for reprinting before my Miscellany) to point out my unhappy Story to the World, with so touching a Humanity, and so good an Effect, that many Persons of Quality, of all Ranks, and of both Sexes, distinguished themselves with the Promptness he had hinted to the noble minded, and not staying till they were applied to, sent me the Honour of their Subscriptions, in the most liberal and handsom Manner, for Encouragement of my Undertaking.

I ought here to acknowledge several Favours from Mr. *Hill*, whose Writings are a shining Ornament of this Miscellany; but I wave detaining my Readers, and beg Leave to refer them to a Copy of Verses called the *Friend*, which I have taken the Liberty to address to that Gentleman.

To return to the Lady, my Mother——Had the celebrated Mr. *Locke* been acquainted with her Example, it had certainly appeared in his *Chapter* against *Innate Practical Principles*; because it would have completed his Instances of Enormities: Some of which, though not exactly in the Order that he mentions them, are as follows——*Have there not been* (says he) *whole Nations, and those of the most civilized People, amongst whom, the exposing their Children, to perish by Want or wild Beasts, has been a Practice as little condemned or scrupled as the begetting them?* Were I inclinable to grow serious, I could easily prove that I have not been more gently dealt with by Mrs. *Bret*; but if this is any way foreign to my Case, I shall find a nearer Example in the whimsical one that ensues.

It is familiar (says the afore-cited Author) *among the* Mengrelians, *a People professing Christianity, to bury their Children alive without*

fess the Truth, with very little* Art. The same Observation may be extended to all his Dedications: his Compliments are constrained and violent, heaped together without the

Scruple——There are indeed sundry Sects of Christians, and I have often wondered which could be my *Mamma's*, but now I find she piously professes and practises Christianity after the Manner of the *Mengrelians*; she industriously obscured me, when my Fortune depended on my being known, and, in that Sense, she may be said to have buried me alive; and sure, like a *Mengrelian*, she must have committed the Action without Scruple; for she is a Woman of Spirit, and can see the Consequence without Remorse——*The* Caribbees (continues my Author) *were wont to castrate their Children in order to fat and eat them*——Here indeed I can draw no Parallel; for to speak but Justice of the Lady, she never contributed ought to have me pampered, but always promoted my being starved: Nor did she, even in my Infancy, betray Fondness enough to be suspected of a Design to devour me; but, on the contrary, not enduring me ever to approach her, offered a Bribe to have had me shipped off, in an odd Manner, to one of the Plantations——When I was about fifteen her Affection began to awake, and had I but known my Interest, I had been handsomly provided for. In short I was solicited to be bound Apprentice to a very honest and reputable Occupation—a *Shoemaker*; an Offer which I undutifully rejected. I was, in fine, unwilling to understand her in a literal Sense, and hoped, that, like the Prophets of old, she might have hinted her Mind in a Kind of Parable, or proverbial Way of speaking; as thus—That one Time or other I might, on due Application, have the Honour of *taking the Length of her Foot.*

Mr. *Locke* mentions *another Set of People that dispatch their Children, if a pretended Astrologer declares them to have unhappy Stars*——Perhaps my *Mamma* has procured some *cunning Man* to calculate my Nativity; or having had some ominous Dream, which preceded my Birth, the dire Event may have appeared to her in the dark and dreary Bottom of a *China* Cup, where Coffee-Stains are often consulted for Prophecies, and held as infallible as were the Leaves of the ancient *Sybils*——To be partly serious: I am rather willing to wrong her Judgment, by suspecting it to be tainted a little with the Tenets of Superstition, than suppose she can be Mistress of a seared Conscience, and act on no Principle at all.

* This the following Extract from it will prove.

—Since our Country has been honour'd with the Glory of your Wit, as elevated and immortal as your Soul, it no longer remains a Doubt whether your Sex have Strength of Mind in Proportion to their Sweetness. There is something in your Verses as distinguished as your Air——They are as strong as Truth, as deep as Reason, as clear as Innocence, and as smooth as Beauty——They contain a nameless and peculiar Mixture of Force and Grace, which is at once so movingly serene, and so majestically lovely, that it is too amiable to appear any where but in your Eyes, and in your Writings.

As Fortune is not more my Enemy than I am the Enemy of Flattery, I know not how I can forbear this Application to your Ladyship, because

Grace of Order, or the Decency of Introduction: he seems to have written his Panegyrics for the Perusal only of his Patrons, and to have imagined that he had no other Task than to pamper them with Praises however gross, and that Flattery would make it's Way to the Heart, without the Assistance of Elegance or Invention.

Soon afterwards the Death of the King furnished a general Subject for a poetical Contest, in which Mr. *Savage* engaged, and is allowed to have carried the Prize of Honour from his Competitors; but I know not whether he gained by his Performance any other Advantage than the Increase of his Reputation; though it must certainly have been with farther Views that he prevailed upon himself to attempt a Species of Writing of which all the Topics had been long before exhausted, and which was made at once difficult by the Multitudes that had failed in it, and those that had succeeded.

He was now advancing in Reputation, and though frequently involved in very distressful Perplexities, appeared however to be gaining upon Mankind, when both his Fame and his Life were endangered by an Event, of which it is not yet determined, whether it ought to be mentioned as a Crime or a Calamity.[25]

On the 20th of *November* 1727, Mr. *Savage* came from *Richmond*, where he then lodged that he might persue his

there is scarce a Possibility that I should say more than I believe, when I am speaking of your Excellence.——

---

[25] Johnson's account of this brawl and its consequences was drawn only in part from his usual sources. For the first part of it, that concerning the crime itself, he relied on the anonymous *Life* supplemented by either *Select Trials . . . at the Session-House in the Old Bailey* (1735) or a similar pamphlet. Savage himself, Johnson said, was unwilling to speak about it (cf. p. 42). For the second part, that concerning the trial, he had also Savage's reminiscences, and for the aftermath he had nothing else, because the anonymous *Life*, which was written as part of a campaign to secure Savage's pardon, stopped short after recording the passing of the death-sentence.

Studies with less Interruption, with an Intent to discharge another Lodging which he had in *Westminster*, and accidentally meeting two Gentlemen his Acquaintances, whose Names were *Merchant* and *Gregory*, he went in with them to a neighbouring Coffee-house, and sat drinking till it was late, it being in no Time of Mr. *Savage*'s Life any Part of his Character to be the first of the Company that desired to separate.[26] He would willingly have gone to Bed in the same House, but there was not Room for the whole Company, and therefore they agreed to ramble about the Streets, and divert themselves with such Amusements as should offer themselves till Morning.

In their Walk they happened unluckily to discover Light in *Robinson*'s Coffee-house, near *Charing-Cross*, and therefore went in. *Merchant* with some Rudeness, demanded a Room, and was told that there was a good Fire in the next Parlour, which the Company were about to leave, being then paying their Reckoning. *Merchant* not satisfied with this Answer, rushed into the Room, and was followed by his Companions. He then petulantly placed himself between the Company and the Fire, and soon after kicked down the Table. This produced a Quarrel, Swords were drawn on both Sides, and one Mr. *James Sinclair* was killed. *Savage* having wounded likewise a Maid that held him, forced his way with *Merchant* out of the House; but being intimidated and confused, without Resolution either to fly or stay, they were taken in a back Court by one of the Company and some Soldiers, whom he had called to his Assistance.

Being secured and guarded that Night, they were in the Morning carried before three Justices, who committed them to the *Gatehouse*, from whence, upon the Death of

[26] In the report of the Coroner's Inquest Savage was described as formerly of the parish of Saint Martin-in-the-Fields, and in the record of their sentences he and his two friends, James Gregory and William Merchant, for whom no addresses are given, were said to possess no goods (Middlesex Record Office).

Mr. *Sinclair*, which happened the same Day, they were removed in the Night to *Newgate*, where they were however treated with some Distinction, exempted from the Ignominy of Chains, and confined, not among the common Criminals, but in the *Press-Yard*.[27]

When the Day of Trial came, the Court was crouded in a very unusual manner, and the Publick appeared to interest itself as in a Cause of general Concern.[28] The Witnesses against Mr. *Savage* and his Friends were, the Woman who kept the House, which was a House of ill Fame, and her Maid, the Men who were in the Room with Mr. *Sinclair*, and a Woman of the Town, who had been drinking with them, and with whom one of them had been seen in Bed. They swore in general, that *Merchant* gave the Provocation, which *Savage* and *Gregory* drew their Swords to justify; that *Savage* drew first, and that he stabbed *Sinclair* when he was not in a Posture of Defence, or while *Gregory* commanded his Sword; that after he had given the Thrust he turned pale, and would have retired, but that the Maid clung round him, and one of the Company endeavoured to detain him, from whom he broke, by cutting the Maid on the Head, but was afterwards taken in a Court.

[27] Sinclair died on 21 Nov. Savage and his two friends were committed to Newgate on the following day 'being charged on Oath with the Murder of James Sinclair' (Calendar of Prisoners in Newgate, Middlesex Record Office). On 23 Nov. a jury empanelled by the Coroner, Robert White, found the three prisoners guilty of homicide. Alterations, however, have been made in parts of both the Calendar and the Inquest. In the former the charge made by the Coroner, which had presumably been murder, has been obliterated and the word 'killing' written in over the blot, and in the latter, notes have been added in English indicating that the jury were discharged from giving any verdict as to Savage and Gregory, and that Merchant was burnt in the hand. Since Merchant's branding was recorded in the Jail Delivery Book under date of 6/7 December 1727, when Savage and Gregory pleaded their pardon, these alterations must have been made then.

[28] A digest of the 'Case of Richard Savage and Gregory' was found among the papers of Alexander Pope (Robert Carruthers, *Life of Alexander Pope* (2nd edn., London, 1857), pp. 424–5). The trial was held at the Old Bailey on Thursday, 7 Dec. 1727.

There was some Difference in their Depositions; one did not see *Savage* give the Wound, another saw it given when *Sinclair* held his Point towards the Ground; and the Woman of the Town asserted, that she did not see *Sinclair*'s Sword at all: This Difference however was very far from amounting to Inconsistency, but it was sufficient to shew, that the Hurry of the Quarrel was such, that it was not easy to discover the Truth with relation to particular Circumstances, and that therefore some Deductions were to be made from the Credibility of the Testimonies.

Sinclair had declared several times before his Death, that he received his Wound from *Savage,* nor did *Savage* at his Trial deny the Fact, but endeavoured partly to extenuate it by urging the Suddenness of the whole Action, and the Impossibility of any ill Design, or premeditated Malice, and partly to justify it by the Necessity of Self-Defence, and the Hazard of his own Life, if he had lost that Opportunity of giving the Thrust: He observed, that neither Reason nor Law obliged a Man to wait for the Blow which was threatned, and which, if he should suffer it, he might never be able to return; that it was always allowable to prevent an Assault, and to preserve Life by taking away that of the Adversary, by whom he was endangered.

With regard to the Violence with which he endeavoured his Escape, he declared, that it was not his Design to fly from Justice, or decline a Trial, but to avoid the Expences and Severities of a Prison, and that he intended to have appeared at the Bar without Compulsion.

This Defence, which took up more that an Hour,[29] was heard by the Multitude that thronged the Court with the most attentive and respectful Silence: Those who thought he ought not to be acquitted owned that Applause could not

[29] Johnson asked Cave to provide him with the text of Savage's defence, but there is no evidence that, if such a document ever existed, Johnson saw it (*Letters of Samuel Johnson*, ed. R. W. Chapman (Oxford, 1952), i. 15).

be refused him; and those who before pitied his Misfortunes, now reverenced his Abilities.

The Witnesses which appeared against him were proved to be Persons of Characters which did not entitle them to much Credit; a common Strumpet, a Woman by whom Strumpets were entertained, and a Man by whom they were supported; and the Character of *Savage* was by several Persons of Distinction asserted, to be that of a modest inoffensive Man, not inclined to Broils, or to Insolence, and who had, to that Time, been only known for his Misfortunes and his Wit.

Had his Audience been his Judges, he had undoubtedly been acquitted; but Mr. *Page*, who was then upon the Bench, treated him with his usual Insolence and Severity, and when he had summed up the Evidence, endeavoured to exasperate the Jury, as Mr. *Savage* used to relate it, with this eloquent Harangue.

Gentlemen of the Jury, you are to consider, that Mr. *Savage* is a very great Man, a much greater Man than you or I, Gentlemen of the Jury; that he wears very fine Clothes, much finer Clothes than you or I, Gentlemen of the Jury; that he has abundance of Money in his Pocket, much more Money than you or I, Gentlemen of the Jury; but, Gentlemen of the Jury, is it not a very hard Case, Gentlemen of the Jury, that Mr. *Savage* should therefore kill you or me, Gentlemen of the Jury?[30]

Mr. *Savage* hearing his Defence thus misrepresented, and

[30] The text of this speech is not found in any of Johnson's documentary sources, and must have come to him either orally or from a manuscript of Savage's. In his reports of the parliamentary debates that he had been writing for the *Gentleman's Magazine*, Johnson had taken a casual attitude towards literal accuracy, and so Sir Francis Page's rhetoric, as reported here, may be indebted considerably to his imagination. Moreover, Johnson may have been influenced by the tradition of Walton and Tacitus, who were accustomed to put speeches into their biographies that can never have been spoken in exactly the form in which they were printed. Yet Page's speech, in the form reported by Johnson, has a more than superficial resemblance to his lordship's usual style, if the sample given in Mark Noble's *Biographical History of England* (1806), iii. 203, is genuine.

the Men who were to decide his Fate incited against him by invidious Comparisons, resolutely asserted, that his Cause was not candidly explained, and began to recapitulate what he had before said with regard to his Condition and the Necessity of endeavouring to escape the Expences of Imprisonment; but the Judge having ordered him to be silent, and repeated his Orders without Effect, commanded that he should be taken from the Bar by Force.

The Jury then heard the Opinion of the Judge, that good Characters were of no Weight against positive Evidence, though they might turn the Scale, where it was doubtful; and that though when two Men attack each other, the Death of either is only Manslaughter; but where one is the Aggressor, as in the Case before them, and in Pursuance of his first Attack, kills the other, the Law supposes the Action, however sudden, to be malicious. They then deliberated upon their Verdict, and determined that Mr. *Savage* and Mr. *Gregory* were guilty of Murder, and Mr. *Merchant*, who had no Sword, only of Manslaughter.[31]

Thus ended this memorable Trial, which lasted eight Hours. Mr. *Savage* and Mr. *Gregory* were conducted back to Prison, where they were more closely confined, and loaded with Irons of fifty Pounds Weight: Four Days afterwards they were sent back to the Court to receive Sentence; on which Occasion Mr. *Savage* made, as far as it could be retained in Memory, the following Speech.

It is now, my Lord, too late to offer any Thing by way of Defence, or Vindication; nor can we expect ought from your Lordships, in this Court, but the Sentence which the Law requires you, as Judges, to pronounce against Men of our calamitous Condition.————But we are also persuaded, that as mere

[31] According to instructions the trial jury found all three prisoners guilty of wilful murder, though the verdict in the case of Merchant must have been later reduced to manslaughter, to agree with the Coroner's verdict. There is no complete official report of the trial—only the Inquest, the Indictment, and the notes in the Calendar of Prisoners and the Jail Delivery Book.

Men, and out of this Seat of rigorous Justice, you are susceptive of the tender Passions, and too humane, not to commiserate the unhappy Situation of those, whom the Law sometimes perhaps ———exacts———from you to pronounce upon. No doubt you distinguish between Offences, which arise out of Premeditation, and a Disposition habituated to Vice or Immorality, and Transgressions, which are the unhappy and unforeseen Effects of a casual Absence of Reason, and sudden Impulse of Passion: We therefore hope you will contribute all you can to an Extension of that Mercy, which the Gentlemen of the Jury have been pleased to shew Mr. *Merchant*, who (allowing Facts as sworn against us by the Evidence) has led us into this our Calamity. I hope, this will not be construed as if we meant to reflect upon that Gentleman, or remove any Thing from us upon him, or that we repine the more at our Fate, because he has no Participation of it: No, my Lord! For my Part, I declare nothing could more soften my Grief, than to be without any Companion in so great a Misfortune*.[32]

Mr. *Savage* had now no Hopes of Life, but from the Mercy of the Crown, which was very earnestly solicited by his Friends, and which, with whatever Difficulty the Story may obtain Belief, was obstructed only by his Mother.

To prejudice the Queen against him, she made use of an Incident, which was omitted in the order of Time, that it might be mentioned together with the Purpose which it was made to serve. Mr. *Savage*, when he had discovered his Birth, had an incessant Desire to speak to his Mother, who always avoided him in publick, and refused him Admission

* Mr. *Savage*'s Life.

[32] This speech is found in both the anonymous *Life* and *Select Trials* with the same lacunae. Both must derive from a common written source. Johnson's statement that he reported it 'as far as it could be retained in the Memory' must mean that it had been extemporaneous and not written down until afterwards. Savage confirmed its accuracy and genuineness (*Memoirs of Mrs. Carter*, p. 60).

At this point the anonymous *Life* breaks off, leaving Johnson from here on without any continuous documentary source of information.

into her House. One Evening walking, as it was his Custom, in the Street that she inhabited, he saw the Door of her House by Accident open; he entered it, and finding none in the Passage, to hinder him, went up Stairs to salute her. She discovered him before he could enter her Chamber, alarmed the Family with the most distressful Outcries, and when she had by her Screams gathered them about her, ordered them to drive out of the House that Villain, who had forced himself in upon her, and endeavoured to murder her. *Savage*, who had attempted with the most submissive Tenderness to soften her Rage, hearing her utter so detestable an Accusation, thought it prudent to retire, and, I believe, never attempted afterwards to speak to her.

But shocked as he was with her Falshood and her Cruelty, he imagined that she intended no other Use of her Lie, than to set herself free from his Embraces and Solicitations, and was very far from suspecting that she would treasure it in her Memory, as an Instrument of future Wickedness, or that she would endeavour for this fictitious Assault to deprive him of his Life.

But when the Queen was solicited for his Pardon, and informed of the severe Treatments which he had suffered from his Judge, she answered, that however unjustifiable might be the Manner of his Trial, or whatever Extenuation the Action for which he was condemned might admit, she could not think that Man a proper Object of the King's Mercy, who had been capable of entering his Mother's House in the Night, with an Intent to murder her.

By whom this atrocious Calumny had been transmitted to the Queen, whether she that invented, had the Front to relate it; whether she found any one weak enough to credit it, or corrupt enough to concur with her in her hateful Design, I know not; but Methods had been taken to persuade the Queen so strongly of the Truth of it, that she for a long Time refused to hear any of those who petitioned for his Life.[33]

Thus had *Savage* perished by the Evidence of a Bawd, a Strumpet, and his Mother, had not Justice and Compassion procured him an Advocate of Rank too great to be rejected unheard, and of Virtue too eminent to be heard without being believed. His Merit and his Calamities happened to reach the Ear of the Countess of *Hertford*, who engaged in his Support with all the Tenderness that is excited by Pity, and all the Zeal which is kindled by Generosity, and demanding an Audience of the Queen, laid before her the whole Series of his Mother's Cruelty, exposed the Improbability of an Accusation by which he was charged with an Intent to commit a Murder, that could produce no Advantage, and soon convinced her how little his former Conduct could deserve to be mentioned as a Reason for extraordinary Severity.

The Interposition of this Lady was so successful, that he was soon after admitted to Bail, and on the 9th of *March* 1728, pleaded the King's Pardon.[34]

It is natural to enquire upon what Motives his Mother could prosecute[35] him in a Manner so outragious and implacable; for what Reason she could employ all the Arts of Malice and all the Snares of Calumny, to take away the Life of her own Son, of a Son who never injured her, who was never supported by her Expence, nor obstructed any Prospect of Pleasure or Advantage; why she should en-

---

[33] Cf. pp. 11–12.

[34] A pardon was ordered on 6 Jan. and passed the seals on 1 Feb. 1728. Savage and Gregory were released on bail on 20 Jan., and pleaded 'the free Pardon of our Lord the King for the pauper Convicts in Newgate' on 28 Feb. 1728. (Endorsement on the Indictment in Middlesex Record Office.) *Select Trials*, p. 250, gave the date as 5 Mar.

[35] 'To *persecute* always implies some cruelty, malignity or injustice; to *prosecute*, is to proceed by legal measures, either with or without just cause' (Johnson's *Dictionary*). At first he had written 'persecute' here, but corrected himself in 1748.

deavour to destroy him by a Lie; a Lie which could not gain Credit, but must vanish of itself at the first Moment of Examination, and of which only this can be said to make it probable, that it may be observed from her Conduct, that the most execrable Crimes are sometimes committed without apparent Temptation.

This Mother is still alive*, and may perhaps even yet, though her Malice was so often defeated, enjoy the Pleasure of reflecting, that the Life which she often endeavoured to destroy, was at least shortened by her maternal Offices; that though she could not transport her Son to the Plantations, bury him in the Shop of a Mechanick, or hasten the Hand of the publick Executioner, she has yet had the Satisfaction of imbittering all his Hours, and forcing him into Exigencies, that hurried on his Death.

It is by no Means necessary to aggravate the Enormity of this Woman's Conduct, by placing it in Opposition to that of the Countess of *Hertford*; no one can fail to observe how much more amiable it is to relieve, than to oppress, and to rescue Innocence from Destruction, than to destroy without an Injury.

Mr. *Savage*, during his Imprisonment, his Trial, and the Time in which he lay under Sentence of Death, behaved with great Firmness and Equality of Mind, and confirmed by his Fortitude the Esteem of those, who before admired him for his Abilities. The peculiar Circumstances of his Life were made more generally known by a short Account†, which was then published, and of which several thousands were in a few Weeks dispersed over the Nation[36]; and the

---

* *Anno* 1743.

† Written by Mr. *Beckingham* and another Gentleman.

---

[36] The anonymous *Life*, Johnson's principal source up to the time of Savage's conviction. Savage said that it had been put together 'from some things I accidentally said in mixed company, and others scattered about at different times in my writings' (*Memoirs of Mrs. Carter*, i. 60). Cf. *AB*, pp. 90–1.

Compassion of Mankind operated so powerfully in his Favour, that he was enabled, by frequent Presents, not only to support himself, but to assist Mr. *Gregory* in Prison; and when he was pardoned and released he found the Number of his Friends not lessened.

The Nature of the Act for which he had been tried was in itself doubtful; of the Evidences which appeared against him, the Character of the Man was not unexceptionable, that of the Women notoriously infamous; she whose Testimony chiefly influenced the Jury to condemn him, afterwards retracted her Assertions. He always himself denied that he was drunk, as had been generally reported. Mr. *Gregory*, who is now Collector of *Antegua*, is said to declare him far less criminal than he was imagined, even by some who favoured him: And *Page* himself afterwards confessed, that he had treated him with uncommon Rigour. When all these Particulars are rated together, perhaps the Memory of *Savage* may not be much sullied by his Trial.

Some Time after he had obtained his Liberty, he met in the Street the Woman that had sworn with so much Malignity against him. She informed him, that she was in Distress, and, with a Degree of Confidence not easily attainable, desired him to relieve her. He, instead of insulting her Misery, and taking Pleasure in the Calamities of one who had brought his Life into Danger, reproved her gently for her Perjury, and changing the only Guinea that he had, divided it equally between her and himself.

This is an Action which in some Ages would have made a Saint, and perhaps in others a Hero, and which, without any hyperbolical Encomiums, must be allowed to be an Instance of uncommon Generosity, an Act of complicated Virtue; by which he at once relieved the Poor, corrected the Vicious, and forgave an Enemy; by which he at once remitted the strongest Provocations, and exercised the most ardent Charity.

Compassion was indeed the distinguishing Quality of *Savage*; he never appeared inclined to take Advantage of Weakness, to attack the defenceless, or to press upon the falling; whoever was distressed was certain at least of his Good-Wishes; and when he could give no Assistance, to extricate them from Misfortunes, he endeavoured to sooth them by Sympathy and Tenderness.

But when his Heart was not softened by the Sight of Misery, he was sometimes obstinate in his Resentment, and did not quickly lose the Remembrance of an Injury. He always continued to speak with Anger of the Insolence and Partiality of *Page*, and a short Time before his Death revenged it by a Satire*.

* The Satire from which the following Lines are extracted was called by Mr. *Savage*, *An Epistle on Authors*: It was never printed intire, but several Fragments were inserted by him in the *Magazine*, after his Retirement into the Country.

> Were all like YORKE of delicate Address,
> Strength to discern, and Sweetness to express;
> Learn'd, just, polite, born ev'ry Heart to gain;
> Like *Cummins* mild, like ᵃ *Fortescue* humane;
> All eloquent of Truth, divinely known;
> So deep, so clear, all Science is his own. [. . .]
>   How far unlike such Worthies, once a Drudge,
> From flound'ring in low Cases, rose a JUDGE.
> Form'd to make Pleaders laugh, his *Nonsense* thunders,
> And, on low Juries, breathes contagious Blunders.
> His Brothers blush, because no Blush he knows,
> Nor e'er ᵇ *one uncorrupted Finger shows*.
> See, drunk with Power, the *Circuit Lord* exprest!
> Full, in his Eye, his Betters stand confest;
> Whose Wealth, Birth, Virtue, from a Tongue so loose,
> 'Scape not provincial, vile, buffoon Abuse.
> Still to what Circuit is assign'd his Name,
> There, swift before him, flies the Warner *Fame*.

ᵃ The Hon. *William Fortescue*, Esq; now Master of the Rolls.
ᵇ When *Page* one uncorrupted Finger shows.
                    D. of *Wharton*.[37]

[37] The second of these notes is Johnson's. The first is Savage's, but Johnson has altered it: Savage had identified Fortescue as '*one of the* Justices *of His* Majesty's *Court of* Common Pleas'.

It is natural to enquire in what Terms Mr. *Savage* spoke of this fatal Action, when the Danger was over, and he was under no Necessity of using any Art to set his Conduct in the fairest Light. He was not willing to dwell upon it, and if he transiently mentioned it, appeared neither to consider himself as a Murderer, nor as a Man wholly free from the Guilt of Blood*. How much and how long he regretted it, appeared in a † Poem which he published many Years

> Contest stops short, Consent yields every Cause
> To Cost, Delay, endures them and withdraws.
> But how 'scape *Pris'ners*? To their Trial chain'd,
> All, all shall stand condemn'd, who stand arraign'd.
> Dire *Guilt*, which else would Detestation cause,
> Pre-judg'd with Insult, wond'rous Pity draws.
> But 'scapes ev'n *Innocence* his harsh Harangue?
> Alas———ev'n Innocence itself must hang;
> Must hang to please him, when of Spleen possest:
> Must hang to bring forth an abortive Jest.
>   Why liv'd he not ere *Star-Chambers* had fail'd,
> When Fine, Tax, Censure, all, but Law, prevail'd;
> Or Law, subservient to some murd'rous Will,
> Became a Precedent to Murder still?
> Yet ev'n when Patriots did for Traytors bleed,
> Was e'er the Jobb to such a Slave decreed;
> Whose savage Mind wants sophist Art to draw,
> O'er murder'd Virtue, specious Veils of Law?
> *Gentleman's Magazine, Sept.* 1741.

* In one of his Letters he stiles it, a *fatal Quarrel, but too well known*

> † Is Chance a Guilt, that my disast'rous Heart,
> For Mischief never meant, must ever smart?
> Can Self-Defence be Sin?—Ah! plead no more;
> What though no purpos'd Malice stain'd thee o'er;
> Had Heav'n befriended thy unhappy Side,
> Thou hadst not been provok'd, or *thou* hadst dy'd.
>   Far be the Guilt of Home-shed Blood from all
> On whom, unsought, embroiling Dangers fall.
> Still the pale *Dead* revives and lives to me,
> To me, through Pity's Eye, condemn'd to see.
> Remembrance veils his Rage, but swells his Fate,
> Griev'd I forgive, and am grown cool too late.
> Young and unthoughtful then, who knows one Day
> What rip'ning Virtues might have made their Way? [. . .]
> He might perhaps his Country's Friend have prov'd,
> Been gen'rous, happy, candid and belov'd;
> He might have sav'd some Worth now doom'd to fall,
> And I perchance in him have *murder'd* all.   *Bastard.*

afterwards.[38] On Occasion of a Copy of Verses in which the Failings of good Men were recounted, and in which the Author had endeavoured to illustrate his Position, that *the best may sometimes deviate from Virtue*, by an Instance of Murder committed by *Savage* in the Heat of Wine, *Savage* remarked, that it was no very just Representation of a good Man, to suppose him liable to Drunkenness, and disposed in his Riots to cut Throats.

He was now indeed at Liberty, but was, as before, without any other Support than accidental Favours and uncertain Patronage afforded him; Sources by which he was sometimes very liberally supplied, and which at other Times were suddenly stopped; so that he spent his Life between Want and Plenty, or what was yet worse, between Beggary and Extravagance; for as whatever he received was the Gift of Chance, which might as well favour him at one Time as another, he was tempted to squander what he had, because he always hoped to be immediately supplied.

Another Cause of his Profusion was the absurd Kindness of his Friends, who at once rewarded and enjoyed his Abilities, by treating him at Taverns, and habituated him to Pleasures which he could not afford to enjoy, and which he was not able to deny himself, though he purchased the Luxury of a single Night by the Anguish of Cold and Hunger for a Week.

The Experience of these Inconveniences determined him to endeavour after some settled Income, which, having long found Submission and Intreaties fruitless, he attempted to extort from his Mother by rougher Methods. He had now, as he acknowledged, lost that Tenderness for her, which the whole Series of her Cruelty had not been able wholly to repress, till he found, by the Efforts which she made for his Destruction, that she was not content with refusing to

---

[38] The *Bastard* was published on 18 Apr. 1728, not 'many Years' but only eight weeks afterwards. Cf. p. 70 and n.

assist him, and being neutral in his Struggles with Poverty, but was as ready to snatch every Opportunity of adding to his Misfortunes, and that she was to be considered as an Enemy implacably malicious, whom nothing but his Blood could satisfy. He therefore threatened to harass her with Lampoons, and to publish a copious Narrative of her Conduct, unless she consented to purchase an Exemption from Infamy, by allowing him a Pension.

This Expedient proved successful. Whether Shame still survived, though Virtue was extinct, or whether her Relations had more Delicacy than herself, and imagined that some of the Darts which Satire might point at her would glance upon them: Lord *Tyrconnel*, whatever were his Motives, upon his Promise to lay aside his Design of exposing the Cruelty of his Mother, received him into his Family, treated him as his Equal, and engaged to allow him a Pension of two hundred Pounds a Year.[39]

This was the Golden Part of Mr. *Savage*'s Life; and for some Time he had no Reason to complain of Fortune; his Appearance was splendid, his Expences large, and his Acquaintance extensive. He was courted by all who endeavoured to be thought Men of Genius, and caressed by all who valued themselves upon a refined Taste. To admire Mr. *Savage* was a Proof of Discernment, and to be acquainted with him was a Title to poetical Reputation. His Presence was sufficient to make any Place of publick Entertainment popular; and his Approbation and Example constituted the Fashion. So powerful is Genius, when it is invested with the Glitter of Affluence; Men willingly pay to Fortune that Regard which they owe to Merit, and are

---

[39] Johnson made this statement in the mistaken belief that the *Bastard* was as yet unpublished. But all of Savage's most merciless attacks on his alleged mother were published whilst he enjoyed his lordship's favour, and at least two must have been written in his house: Preface to *Miscellaneous Poems* (1726/8), the *Bastard* (1728), the *Wanderer* (1729).

Lord Tyrconnel took a major part in securing Savage's pardon. They did not quarrel until 1735. Cf. p. 59 and *AB*, p. 96.

pleased when they have an Opportunity at once of grati-
fying their Vanity, and practising their Duty.

This Interval of Prosperity furnished him with Opportunities of enlarging his Knowledge of human Nature, by
contemplating Life from it's highest Gradations to it's
lowest, and had he afterwards applied to Dramatic Poetry, he
would perhaps not have had many Superiors; for as he never
suffered any Scene to pass before his Eyes without Notice,
he had treasured in his Mind all the different Combinations
of Passions, and the innumerable Mixtures of Vice and
Virtue, which distinguish one Character from another; and
as his Conception was strong, his Expressions were clear, he
easily received Impressions from Objects, and very forcibly
transmitted them to others.

Of his exact Observations on human Life he has left a
Proof, which would do Honour to the greatest Names, in a
small Pamphlet, called, *The Author to be let*, where he
introduces *Iscariot Hackney*, a prostitute Scribler, giving
an Account of his Birth, his Education, his Disposition and
Morals, Habits of Life and Maxims of Conduct. In the
Introduction are related many secret Histories of the petty
Writers of that Time, but sometimes mixed with ungenerous
Reflections on their Birth, their Circumstances, or those of
their Relations; nor can it be denied, that some Passages are
such as *Iscariot Hackney* might himself have produced.

He was accused likewise of living in an Appearance of
Friendship with some whom he satirised, and of making use
of the Confidence which he gained by a seeming Kindness
to discover Failings and expose them; it must be confessed,
that Mr. *Savage*'s Esteem was no very certain Possession,
and that he would lampoon at one Time those whom he
had praised at another.

It may be alledged, that the same Man may change his
Principles, and that he who was once deservedly commended, may be afterwards satirised with equal Justice, or

that the Poet was dazzled with the Appearance of Virtue, and found the Man whom he had celebrated, when he had an Opportunity of examining him more nearly, unworthy of the Panegyric which he had too hastily bestowed; and that as a false Satire ought to be recanted, for the sake of him whose Reputation may be injured, false Praise ought likewise to be obviated, lest the Distinction between Vice and Virtue should be lost, lest a bad Man should be trusted upon the Credit of his Encomiast, or lest others should endeavour to obtain the like Praises by the same Means.

But though these Excuses may be often plausible, and sometimes just, they are very seldom satisfactory to Mankind; and the Writer, who is not constant to his Subject, quickly sinks into Contempt, his Satire loses its Force, and his Panegyric its Value, and he is only considered at one Time as a Flatterer, and as a Calumniator at another.

To avoid these Imputations, it is only necessary to follow the Rules of Virtue, and to preserve an unvaried Regard to Truth. For though it is undoubtedly possible, that a Man, however cautious, may be sometimes deceived by an artful Appearance of Virtue, or by false Evidences of Guilt, such Errors will not be frequent; and it will be allowed, that the Name of an Author would never have been made contemptible, had no Man ever said what he did not think, or misled others, but when he was himself deceived.

The *Author to be let* was first published in a single Pamphlet, and afterwards inserted in a Collection of Pieces relating to the *Dunciad*, which were addressed by Mr. *Savage* to the Earl of *Middlesex*, in a * Dedication, which he was

---

* *To the right honourable the Earl of* Middlesex.

My LORD,
That elegant Taste in Poetry, which is hereditary to your Lordship, together with that particular Regard, with which you honour the Author to whom these Papers relate, make me imagine this Collection may not be unpleasing to you. And I may presume to say, the Pieces themselves are

prevailed upon to sign, though he did not write it, and in which there are some Positions, that the true Author[40] would perhaps not have published under his own Name; and on

such as are not unworthy your Lordship's Patronage, my own Part in it excepted. I speak only of the *Author to be let*, having no Title to any other, not even the small ones out of the Journals. May I be permitted to declare (to the end I may seem not quite so unworthy of your Lordship's Favour, as some Writers of my *Age* and Circumstances) that I never was concerned in any Journals. I ever thought the exorbitant Liberty, which most of those Papers take with their Superiors, unjustifiable in any Rank of Men; but detestable in such who do it merely for Hire, and without even the bad Excuse of *Passion* and *Resentment*. On the contrary, being once inclined, upon some advantageous Proposals, to enter into a [a] Paper of another Kind, I immediately desisted, on finding admitted into it (though as the Publisher told me purely by an Accident) two or three Lines reflecting on a *great Minister*. Were my Life ever so unhappy, it shall not be stained with a Conduct, which my Birth at least (though neither my *Education* nor *good Fortune*) should set me above, much less with any Ingratitude to that noble Person, to whose Intercession (next to his Majesty's Goodness) I owe in a great Measure that *Life itself*.

———*Nec si miserum Fortuna Sinonem*
Finxit, vanum etiam mendacemque improba finget.

I believe your Lordship will pardon this Digression, or any other which keeps me from the Stile, you so much hate, of Dedication.

I will not pretend to display those rising Virtues in your Lordship, which the next Age will certainly know without my Help, but rather relate (what else it will as certainly be ignorant of) the History of these Papers, and the Occasion which produced the *War of the Dunces*, (for so it has been commonly called) which begun in the Year 1727, and ended in 1730.

When Dr. *Swift* and Mr. *Pope* thought it proper, for Reasons specified in the Preface to their Miscellanies, to publish such little Pieces of theirs as had casually got abroad, there was added to them the Treatise of the *Bathos, or the Art of Sinking in Poetry*. It happened that in one Chapter of this Piece, the several Species of bad Poets were ranged in Classes, to which were prefixed almost all the Letters of the Alphabet (the greatest

---

[a] The Paper here meant, was probably the *Grubstreet-Journal*, which Mr. *Savage* was once invited to undertake, but which he declined, whether for the Reason here mentioned is not certain.[41]

---

[40] Johnson believed the 'true Author' to have been Pope. *Lives of the Poets*, ed. G. B. Hill (Oxford, 1905), iii. 147. The motives that may have led Johnson to avoid Pope's name here have been discussed in the Textual Introduction. But the name is mentioned frequently in Savage's Dedication (printed in Johnson's note) and several times subsequently in Johnson's own text; cf. p. 110 and n.

[41] This footnote is Johnson's.

47

which Mr. *Savage* afterwards reflected with no great Satisfaction.

The Enumeration of the bad Effects of the *uncontrolled*

Part of them at Random) but such was the Number of Poets eminent in *that Art*, that some one or other took every Letter to himself: All fell into so violent a Fury, that for half a Year, or more, the common *News-Papers* (in most of which they had some Property, as being *hired Writers*) were filled with the most abusive Falshoods and Scurrilities they could possibly devise. A Liberty no Way to be wondered at in those People, and in those Papers, that, for many Years during the uncontrolled License of the Press, had aspersed almost all the great *Characters* of the Age; and this with Impunity, their own *Persons* and *Names* being utterly secret and obscure.

This gave Mr. *Pope* the Thought, that he had now some Opportunity of doing Good, by detecting and dragging into Light these common Enemies of Mankind; since to *invalidate* this universal Slander, it sufficed to shew what contemptible Men were the Authors of it. He was not without Hopes, that by manifesting the Dulness of those who had only Malice to recommend them, either the Booksellers would not find their Account in employing them, or the Men themselves when discovered, want Courage to proceed in so unlawful an Occupation. This it was that gave Birth to the *Dunciad*, and he thought it an Happiness, that by the late Flood of Slander on himself, he had acquired such a peculiar Right over their *Names* as was necessary to this Design.

On the 12th of *March* 1729, at St. *James*'s, that Poem was presented to the KING and QUEEN (who had before been pleased to read it) by the right honourable Sir *Robert Walpole*: And some Days after the whole Impression was taken and dispersed by several Noblemen and Persons of the first Distinction.

It is certainly a true Observation, that no People are so impatient of Censure as those who are the greatest Slanderers: Which was wonderfully exemplified on this Occasion. On the Day the Book was first vended, a Crowd of Authors besieged the Shop; Entreaties, Advices, Threats of Law, and Battery, nay Cries of Treason were all employed to hinder the coming out of the *Dunciad*: On the other side the Booksellers and Hawkers made as great Efforts to procure it: What could a few poor Authors do against so great a Majority as the Publick? There was no stopping a Torrent with a Finger, so out it came.

Many ludicrous Circumstances attended it: The Dunces (for by this Name they were called) held weekly Clubs, to consult of Hostilities against the Author; one wrote a Letter to a great Minister, assuring him Mr. *Pope* was the greatest Enemy the Government had; and another bought his Image in Clay, to execute him in Effigy; with which sad Sort of Satisfactions the Gentlemen were a little comforted.

Some false Editions of the Book having an Owl in their Frontispiece, the true one, to distinguish it, fixed in its stead an Ass laden with Authors. Then another surreptitious one being printed with the same Ass, the new Edition in Octavo returned for Distinction to the Owl again. Hence arose a great Contest of Booksellers against Booksellers, and Advertisements

Freedom of the Press, and the Assertion that the *Liberties taken by the Writers of Journals with their Superiors were exorbitant and unjustifiable*, very ill became Men, who have themselves not always shewn the exactest Regard to the Laws of Subordination in their Writings, and who have often satirised those that at least thought themselves their Superiors, as they were eminent for their hereditary Rank, and employed in the highest Offices of the Kingdom. But this is only an Instance of that Partiality which almost every Man indulges with Regard to himself; the Liberty of the Press is a Blessing when we are inclined to write against others, and a Calamity when we find ourselves overborn by the Multitude of our Assailants; as the Power of the Crown is always thought too great by those who suffer by it's Influence, and too little by those in whose Favour it is exerted; and a Standing Army is generally accounted necessary by those who command, and dangerous and oppressive by those who support it.

Mr. *Savage* was likewise very far from believing, that the Letters annexed to each Species of bad Poets in the *Bathos*, were, as he was directed to assert, *set down at*

against Advertisements; some recommending the *Edition of the Owl*, and others the *Edition of the Ass*; by which Names they came to be distinguished, to the great Honour also of the Gentlemen of the *Dunciad*.

Your Lordship will not think these Particulars altogether unentertaining; nor are they impertinent, since they clear some Passages in the following Collection. The whole cannot but be of some Use, to shew the *different Spirit* with which good and bad Authors have ever *acted*, as well as *written*; and to evince a Truth, a greater than which was never advanced, that——

Each bad Author is as bad a Friend.

However, the Imperfection of this Collection cannot but be owned, as long as it wants that Poem with which you, my Lord, have honoured the Author of the *Dunciad*; but which I durst not presume to add in your Absence. As it is, may it please your Lordship to accept of it, as a distant Testimony, with what Respect and Zeal I am,

My Lord,
your most obedient
and devoted Servant,
R. Savage.

Random; for when he was charged by one of his Friends with putting his Name to such an Improbability, he had no other Answer to make, than that *he did not think of it*, and his Friend had too much Tenderness to reply, that next to the Crime of writing contrary to what he thought, was that of writing without thinking.

After having remarked what is false in this Dedication, it is proper that I observe the Impartiality which I recommend, by declaring what *Savage* asserted, that the Account of the Circumstances which attended the Publication of the *Dunciad*, however strange and improbable, was exactly true.

The Publication of this Piece at this Time raised Mr. *Savage* a great Number of Enemies among those that were attacked by Mr. *Pope*, with whom he was considered as a Kind of Confederate, and whom he was suspected of supplying with private Intelligence and secret Incidents: So that the Ignominy of an Informer was added to the Terror of a Satirist.

That he was not altogether free from literary Hypocrisy, and that he sometimes spoke one thing, and wrote another, cannot be denied, because he himself confessed, that when he lived in great Familiarity with *Dennis*, he wrote an Epigram * against him.[42]

---

* *This Epigram was, I believe, never published.*

> Should *Dennis* publish you had stabb'd your Brother,
> Lampoon'd your Monarch, or debauch'd your Mother;
> Say what Revenge on *Dennis* can be had,
> Too dull for Laughter, for Reply too mad?
> On one so poor you cannot take the Law,
> On one so old your Sword you scorn to draw:
> Uncag'd, then let the harmless Monster rage,
> Secure in Dulness, Madness, Want, and Age.

---

[42] Johnson's statement that this epigram was by Savage and that it had not been published is odd because it had already appeared in print three times (*Grub-street Journal*, no. 78, 1 July 1731; *GM*. 31, 306; *Memoirs of the Society of Grub-street*, 1737), and in the *Memoirs* it had been marked 'A', the symbol regularly employed to indicate Pope's authorship. But since Johnson's version is different, he must have had an independent source, either his memory or a manuscript perhaps in Savage's hand.

Mr. *Savage* however set all the Malice of all the pigmy Writers at Defiance, and thought the Friendship of Mr. *Pope* cheaply purchased by being exposed to their Censure and their Hatred; nor had he any Reason to repent of the Preference, for he found Mr. *Pope* a steady and unalienable Friend almost to the End of his Life.

About this Time, notwithstanding his avowed Neutrality with regard to Party, he published a Panegyric on Sir *Robert Walpole*, for which he was rewarded by him with twenty Guineas, a Sum not very large, if either the Excellence of the Performance, or the Wealth of the Patron be considered; but greater than he afterwards obtained from a Person of yet higher Rank, and more desirous in Appearance of being distinguished as a Patron of Literature.

As he was very far from approving the Conduct of Sir *Robert Walpole*, and in Conversation mentioned him sometimes with Acrimony, and generally with Contempt, as he was one of those who were always zealous in their Assertions of the Justice of the late Opposition, jealous of the Rights of the People, and alarmed by the long continued Triumph of the Court; it was natural to ask him what could induce him to employ his Poetry in Praise of that Man who was, in his Opinion, an Enemy to Liberty, and an Oppressor of his Country? He alleged, that he was then dependent upon the Lord *Tyrconnel*, who was an implicite Follower of the Ministry, and that being enjoined by him, not without Menaces, to write in Praise of his Leader, he had not Resolution sufficient to sacrifice the Pleasure of Affluence to that of Integrity.

In 1751 Warburton published it as Pope's in vol. v of the *Works of Alexander Pope*, p. 88 (large 8vo edn. only), but he used Johnson's version of the text rather than the *Grub-street* one. His ascription of authorship to Pope is undoubtedly correct.

No other epigram on Dennis by Savage is known to exist, except for a couplet added to a poem signed 'J.D.' (= John Dennis) when it was reprinted in the *Grub-street Journal* in 1733:

> I'm glad to find my *brother's* grateful lay,
> *Like medlar fruit, delicious in decay.*

On this and on many other Occasions he was ready to lament the Misery of living at the Tables of other Men, which was his Fate from the Beginning to the End of his Life; for I know not whether he ever had, for three Months together, a fettled Habitation, in which he could claim a Right of Residence.

To this unhappy State it is just to impute much of the Inconstancy of his Conduct; for though a Readiness to comply with the Inclination of others was no Part of his natural Character,[43] yet he was sometimes obliged to relax his Obstinacy, and submit his own Judgment and even his Virtue to the Government of those by whom he was supported: So that if his Miseries were sometimes the Consequence of his Faults, he ought not yet to be wholly excluded from Compassion, because his Faults were very often the Effects of his Misfortunes.

In this gay Period* of his Life, while he was supported by Affluence and Pleasure, he published the *Wanderer*, a moral Poem of which the Design is comprised in these Lines:

> I fly all public Care, all venal Strife,
> To try the *still* compar'd with *active Life*,
> To prove by these, the Sons of Men may owe
> The Fruits of Bliss to bursting Clouds of Woe;
> That even Calamity by Thought refin'd
> Inspirits and adorns the thinking Mind.

and more distinctly in the following Passage;

> By Woe the Soul to daring Action swells,
> By Woe in plaintless Patience it excels;
> From Patience prudent, clear Experience springs,
> And traces Knowledge through the Course of Things.
> Thence Hope is form'd, thence Fortitude, Success,
> Renown—whate'er Men covet and caress.

* 1729.

[43] This does not seem consistent with what Johnson observed on p. 136: 'He had the Art of escaping from his own Reflections and accomodating himself to every new Scene.'

This Performance was always considered by himself as his Master-piece, and Mr. *Pope*, when he was asked his Opinion of it, told him, that he read it once over, and was not displeased with it, that it gave him more Pleasure at the second Perusal, and delighted him still more at the third.

It has been generally objected to the *Wanderer*, that the Disposition of the Parts is irregular, that the Design is obscure, and the Plan perplexed, that the Images, however beautiful, succeed each other without Order; and that the whole Performance is not so much a regular Fabric as a Heap of shining Materials thrown together by Accident, which strikes rather with the solemn Magnificence of a stupendous Ruin, than the elegant Grandeur of a finished Pile.

This Criticism is universal, and therefore it is reasonable to believe it at least in a great Degree just; but Mr. *Savage* was always of a contrary Opinion; he thought his Drift could only be missed by Negligence or Stupidity, and that the whole Plan was regular, and the Parts distinct.

It was never denied to abound with strong Representations of Nature, and just Observations upon Life, and it may easily be observed, that most of his Pictures have an evident Tendency to illustrate his first great Position, *that Good is the Consequence of Evil*. The Sun that burns up the Mountains, fructifies the Vales, the Deluge that rushes down the broken Rocks with dreadful Impetuosity, is separated into purling Brooks; and the Rage of the Hurricane purifies the Air.

Even in this Poem he has not been able to forbear one Touch upon the Cruelty of his Mother*, which though

---

* False Pride! what Vices on our Conduct steal
From the World's Eye one Frailty to conceal.
Ye cruel Mothers—soft! these Words command—
So near should *Cruelty* and *Mother* stand? [...]
Can the fond Goat, or tender fleecy Dam
Howl like the Wolf to tear the Kid or Lamb?
Yes, there are Mothers——there I fear'd his Aim,
And conscious trembl'd at the coming Name:

remarkably delicate and tender, is a Proof how deep an Impression it had made upon his Mind.

This must be at least acknowledged, which ought to be thought equivalent to many other Excellencies, that this Poem can promote no other Purposes than those of Virtue, and that it is written with a very strong Sense of the Efficacy of Religion.

But my Province is rather to give the History of Mr. *Savage's* Performances, than to display their Beauties, or to obviate the Criticisms, which they have occasioned, and therefore I shall not dwell upon the particular Passages which deserve Applause: I shall neither show the Excellence of his Descriptions*, nor expatiate on the terrific Portrait

> Then with a Sigh his issuing Words oppos'd,
> Straight with a falling Tear his Speech he clos'd;
> That Tenderness which ties of Blood deny,
> Nature repaid me from a Stranger's Eye.
> Pale grow my Cheeks——

* *Of his Descriptions this Specimen may be offered.*

> Now, from yon Range of Rocks, strong Rays rebound,
> Doubling the Day on flow'ry Plains around:
> *Kingcups* beneath far-striking Colours glance,
> Bright as th' etherial glows the green Expanse.
> Gems of the Field!——The Topaz charms the Sight,
> Like these, effulging yellow Streams of Light.
> From the same Rocks fall Rills with soften'd Force,
> Meet in yon Mead, and well a River's Source.
> Through her clear Channel shine her finny Shoals,
> O'er Sands like Gold the liquid Crystal rolls.
> Dim'd in yon coarser Moor her Charms decay,
> And shape through rustling Reeds a ruffled Way.
> Near Willows short and bushy Shadows throw:
> Now lost she seems through nether Tracts to flow;
> Yet at yon Point winds out in Silver State,
> Like Virtue from a Labyrinth of Fate.
> In length'ning Rows prone from the Mountains run
> The Flocks:—Their Fleeces glist'ning in the Sun;
> Her Streams they seek, and, 'twixt her neighb'ring Trees.
> Recline in various Attitudes of Ease:
> Where the Herds sip, the little scaly Fry,
> Swift from the Shore, in scatt'ring Myriads fly.
> Each liv'ried Cloud, that round th' Horizon glows,
> Shifts in odd Scenes, like Earth from whence it rose.

of *Suicide**, nor point out the artful Touches†, by which
he has distinguished the intellectual Features of the Rebels,
who suffer Death in his last Canto. It is, however, proper to

> The Bee hums wanton in yon Jess'mine Bower,
> And circling settles, and despoils the Flower.
> Melodious there the plumy Songsters meet,
> And call charm'd Echo from her arch'd Retreat.
> Neat, polish'd Mansions rise in Prospect gay;
> Time-batter'd Tow'rs frown awful in Decay:
> The Sun plays glitt'ring on the Rocks and Spires,
> And the Lawn lightens with reflected Fires.

* *Who in the second Canto is thus introduced.*

> Now Grief and Rage, by gath'ring Sighs supprest,
> Swell my full Heart, and heave my lab'ring Breast!
> With struggling Starts each vital String they strain,
> And strike the tott'ring Fabric of my Brain!
> O'er my sunk Spirits frowns a vap'ry Scene,
> Woe's dark Retreat! the madding Maze of Spleen!
> A deep, damp Gloom o'erspreads the murky Cell;
> Here pining Thoughts, and secret Terrors dwell!
> Here learn the Great unreal Wants to feign!
> Unpleasing Truths here mortify the Vain!
> Here Learning, blinded first, and then beguil'd,
> Looks dark as Ignorance, as Frenzy wild!
> Here first Credulity on Reason won!
> And here *false Zeal* mysterious Rants begun!
> Here *Love* impearls each Moment with a Tear,
> And *Superstition* owes to *Spleen* her Fear!
> ——Here the lone Hour, a Blank of Life, displays,
> Till now bad Thoughts a Fiend more active raise;
> A Fiend in evil Moments ever nigh!
> Death in her Hand, and Frenzy in her Eye!
> Her Eye all red, and sunk! A Robe she wore,
> With Life's Calamities embroider'd o'er.
> A Mirror in one Hand collective shows,
> Varied, and multiplied, that group of Woes.
> This endless Foe to gen'rous Toil and Pain
> Lolls on a Couch for Ease; but lolls in vain;
> She muses o'er her Woe-embroidered Vest,
> And Self-abhorrence heightens in her Breast.
> To shun her Care, the Force of Sleep she tries,
> Still wakes her Mind, though Slumbers doze her Eyes:
> She dreams, starts, rises, stalks from Place to Place,
> With restless, thoughtful, interrupted Pace:
> Now eyes the Sun, and curses ev'ry Ray,
> Now the green Ground, where Colour fades away.

[*Note* * *cont. and note* † *on p. 56*]

observe, that Mr. *Savage* always declared the Characters wholly fictitious, and without the least Allusion to any real Persons or Actions.

> Dim Spectres dance! Again her Eye she rears;
> Then from the Blood-shot Ball wipes purpled Tears;
> Then presses hard her Brow, with Mischief fraught,
> Her Brow half bursts with Agony of Thought!
> From me (she cries) pale Wretch thy Comfort claim,
> Born of Despair, and *Suicide* my Name!

† *His three Rebels are thus described.*

> Of these were three by different Motives fir'd,
> Ambition one, and one Revenge inspir'd.
> The third, O Mammon, was thy meaner Slave;
> Thou Idol seldom of the Great and Brave.
>   *Florio,* whose Life was one continued Feast,
> His Wealth diminish'd, and his Debts encreas'd,
> Vain Pomp and Equipage his low Desires,
> Who ne'er to intellectual Bliss aspires;
> He, to repair by Vice what Vice has broke,
> Durst with bold Treasons Judgment's Rod provoke.
> His Strength of Mind, by Lux'ry half dissolv'd,
> Ill Brooks the Woe where deep he stands involv'd.
> ——His Genius flies; reflects he now on Prayer?
> Alas! bad Spirits turn those Thoughts to Air.
> What shall be next? What? strait relinquish Breath,
> To bar a public, just tho' shameful Death?
> Rash, horrid Thought! yet now afraid to live,
> Murd'rous he strikes; may Heav'n the Deed forgive!
> ——Why had he thus false Spirit to rebel?
> And why not Fortitude to suffer well?
>   ——Where no kind Lips the hallow'd Dirge resound,
> Far from the Compass of yon sacred Ground;
> Full in the Center of three meeting Ways,
> Stak'd through he lies——Warn'd let the Wicked gaze!
>   Near yonder Fane where Mis'ry sleeps in Peace,
> Whose Spire fast-lessens, as these Shades encrease,
> Left to the North, whence oft brew'd Tempests roll,
> Tempests, dire Emblems, *Cosmo,* of thy Soul!
> There! mark that *Cosmo* much for Guile renown'd!
> His Grave by unbid Plants of Poison crown'd.
> When out of Pow'r, through him the public Good,
> So strong his factious Tribe, suspended stood.
> In Power, vindictive Actions were his Aim,
> And Patriots perish'd by th' ungenerous Flame.
> If the best Cause he in the Senate chose,
> Ev'n Right in him from some wrong Motive rose.
> The Bad he loath'd, and would the Weak despise!
> Yet courted for dark Ends, and shun'd the Wise.

From a Poem so diligently laboured, and so successfully
finished, it might be reasonably expected that he should have
gained considerable Advantage; nor can it, without some

> When ill his Purpose, eloquent his Strain,
> His Malice had a Look and Voice humane:
> His Smile the Signal of some vile Intent,
> A private Ponyard, or empoison'd Scent;
> Proud, yet to popular Applause a Slave;
> No Friend he honour'd, and no Foe forgave.
> His Boons unfrequent, or unjust to need,
> The Hire of Guilt, of Infamy the Meed;
> But if they chanc'd on learned Worth to fall,
> Bounty in him was Ostentation all.
> No true Benevolence his Thought sublimes,
> His noblest Actions are illustrious Crimes.
> ——*Cosmo*, as Death draws nigh, no more conceals
> That Storm of Passions, which his Nature feels;
> He feels much Fear, more Anger, and most Pride;
> But Pride and Anger make all Fear subside.
> Dauntless he meets at length untimely Fate;
> A desp'rate Spirit! rather fierce, than great.
> Darkling he glides along the dreary Coast,
> A sullen, wand'ring, self-tormenting Ghost.
> ——Where veiny Marble dignifies the Ground,
> With Emblem fair in Sculpture rising round,
> Just where a crossing, length'ning Isle we find,
> Full East; whence God returns to judge Mankind,
> Once lov'd *Horatio* sleeps, a Mind elate!
> Lamented Shade, Ambition was thy Fate!
> Ev'n Angels, wond'ring, oft his Worth survey'd;
> *Behold a Man like one of us!* they said.
> Straight heard the Furies, and with Envy glar'd,
> And to precipitate his Fall prepar'd:
> First *Av'rice* came. In vain Self-love she press'd;
> The Poor he pitied still, and still redress'd:
> Learning was his, and Knowledge to commend,
> Of Arts a Patron, and of Want a Friend.
> Next came *Revenge*: But her Essay, how vain?
> Nor Hate nor Envy in his Heart remain:
> No previous Malice could his Mind engage,
> Malice the Mother of vindictive Rage.
> No——from his Life his Foes might learn to live;
> He held it still a Triumph to forgive.
> At length *Ambition* urg'd his Country's Weal,
> Assuming the fair Look of public *Zeal*;
> Still in his Breast so gen'rous glow'd the Flame,
> The Vice, when there, a Virtue half became.
> His pitying Eye saw Millions in Distress,
> He deem'd it God-like to have Pow'r to bless;

Degree of Indignation and Concern, be told that he sold the Copy for ten Guineas, of which he afterwards returned two, that the two last Sheets of the Work might be reprinted, of which he had in his Absence intrusted the Correction to a Friend, who was too indolent to perform it with Accuracy.

A superstitious Regard to the Correction of his Sheets was one of Mr. *Savage*'s Peculiarities; he often altered, revised, recurred to his first Reading or Punctuation, and again adopted the Alteration; he was dubious and irresolute without End, as on a Question of the last Importance, and at last was seldom satisfied; the Intrusion or Omission of a Comma was sufficient to discompose him, and he would lament an Error of a single Letter as a heavy Calamity. In one of his Letters relating to an Impression of some Verses he remarks, that he had with regard to the Correction of the Proof *a Spell upon him*, and indeed the Anxiety, with which he dwelt upon the minutest and most trifling Niceties, deserved no other Name than that of Fascination.

That he sold so valuable a Performance for so small a Price was not to be imputed either to Necessity by which the Learned and Ingenious are often obliged to submit to very hard Conditions, or to Avarice by which the Booksellers are frequently incited to oppress that Genius by which they are supported, but to that intemperate Desire of Pleasure, and habitual Slavery to his Passions, which involved him in many Perplexities; he happened at that Time to be engaged in the Pursuit of some trifling Gratification, and being without Money for the present Occasion, sold his Poem to the first Bidder, perhaps for the first Price that

> Thus, when unguarded, Treason stain'd him o'er,
> And Virtue and Content were then no more.
>   But when to Death by rig'rous Justice doom'd,
> His genuine Spirit Saint-like State resum'd.
> Oft from soft Penitence distill'd a Tear;
> Oft Hope in heav'nly Mercy lighten'd Fear;
> Oft would a Drop from struggling Nature fall,
> And then a Smile of Patience brighten all.

was proposed, and would probably have been content with less, if less had been offered him.

This Poem was addressed to the Lord *Tyrconnel* not only in the first Lines*, but in a formal Dedication filled with the highest Strains of Panegyric, and the warmest Professions of Gratitude, but by no Means remarkable for Delicacy of Connection or Elegance of Stile.

These Praises in a short Time he found himself inclined to retract, being discarded by the Man on whom he had bestowed them, and whom he then immediately discovered not to have deserved them.[44] Of this Quarrel, which every Day made more bitter, Lord *Tyrconnel* and Mr. *Savage* assigned very different Reasons, which might perhaps all in Reality concur, though they were not all convenient to be alleged by either Party. Lord *Tyrconnel* affirmed, that it was the constant Practice of Mr. *Savage*, to enter a Tavern with any Company that proposed it, drink the most expensive Wines, with great Profusion, and when the Reckoning was demanded, to be without Money: If, as it often happened, his Companions were willing to defray his Part, the Affair ended, without any ill Consequences; but if they were refractory, and expected that the Wine should be paid for by him that drank it, his Method of Composition was, to take them with him to his own Apartment, assume the Government of the House, and order the Butler in an

* Fain would my Verse, *Tyrconnel*, boast thy Name,
  Brownlow at once my Subject, and my Fame:
  O could that Spirit which thy Bosom warms,
  Whose Strength surprises, and whose Goodness charms,
  Thy various Worth—could that inspire my Lays,
  Envy should smile, and Censure learn to praise:
  Yet though unequal to a Soul like thine,
  A gen'rous Soul approaching to divine;
  While bless'd beneath such Patronage I write,
  Great my Attempt, though hazardous my Flight.

---

[44] In 1735; cf. *AB*, pp. 129–30.

imperious Manner to set the best Wine in the Cellar before his Company, who often drank till they forgot the Respect due to the House in which they were entertained, indulged themselves in the utmost Extravagance of Merriment, practised the most licentious Frolics, and committed all the Outrages of Drunkenness.

Nor was this the only Charge which Lord *Tyrconnel* brought against him: Having given him a Collection of valuable Books, stamped with his own Arms, he had the Mortification to see them in a short Time exposed to Sale upon the Stalls, it being usual with Mr. *Savage*, when he wanted a small Sum, to take his Books to the Pawnbroker.

Whoever was acquainted with Mr. *Savage*, easily credited both these Accusations; for having been obliged from his first Entrance into the World to subsist upon Expedients, Affluence was not able to exalt him above them; and so much was he delighted with Wine and Conversation, and so long had he been accustomed to live by Chance, that he would at any time go to the Tavern, without Scruple, and trust for his Reckoning to the Liberality of his Company, and frequently of Company to whom he was very little known. This Conduct indeed very seldom drew upon him those Inconveniences that might be feared by any other Person, for his Conversation was so entertaining, and his Address so pleasing, that few thought the Pleasure which they received from him dearly purchased by paying for his Wine. It was his peculiar Happiness, that he scarcely ever found a Stranger, whom he did not leave a Friend; but it must likewise be added, that he had not often a Friend long, without obliging him to become a Stranger.

Mr. *Savage*, on the other Hand, declared, that Lord *Tyrconnel* * quarrelled with him, because he would not

* His Expression in one of his Letters, was, that Lord *T——l* had involved his *Estate, and therefore poorly sought an Occasion to quarrel with him.*

substract[45] from his own Luxury and Extravagance what he had promised to allow him, and that his Resentment was only a Plea for the Violation of his Promise: He asserted that he had done nothing that ought to exclude him from that Subsistence which he thought not so much a Favour, as a Debt, since it was offered him upon Conditions, which he had never broken; and that his only Fault was, that he could not be supported with nothing.

He acknowledged, that Lord *Tyrconnel* often exhorted him to regulate his Method of Life, and not to spend all his Nights in Taverns, and that he appeared very desirous, that he would pass those Hours with him which he so freely bestowed upon others. This Demand Mr. *Savage* considered as a Censure of his Conduct, which he could never patiently bear; and which even in the latter and cooler Part of his Life was so offensive to him, that he declared it as his Resolution, *to spurn that Friend who should presume to dictate to him*; and it is not likely, that in his earlier Years he received Admonitions with more Calmness.

He was likewise inclined to resent such Expectations, as tending to infringe his Liberty, of which he was very jealous when it was necessary to the Gratification of his Passions, and declared, that the Request was still more unreasonable, as the Company to which he was to have been confined was insupportably disagreeable. This Assertion affords another Instance of that Inconsistency of his Writings with his Conversation, which was so often to be observed. He forgot how lavishly he had, in his * Dedication to the WANDERER,

* Part of this Poem had the Honour of your Lordship's Perusal when in Manuscript, and it was no small Pride to me when it met with Approbation.—My Intention [. . .] is to embrace this Opportunity of throwing out Sentiments that relate to your Lordship's Goodness and Generosity, which give me leave to say I have lately experienced. [. . .]

[45] Johnson considered the spellings *substract* and *subtract* alternatives, the former being the more common (*Dictionary*). Five of the early editions (44, 75, 79–81, 81, 83) used the former, and the remainder the latter spelling.

extolled the Delicacy and Penetration, the Humanity and Generosity, the Candour and Politeness of the Man, whom, when he no longer loved him, he declared to be a Wretch without Understanding, without Good-Nature, and without Justice; of whose Name he thought himself obliged to leave no Trace in any future Edition of his Writings; and accordingly blotted it out of that Copy of the *Wanderer* which was in his Hands.

During his Continuance with the Lord *Tyrconnel*[46] he wrote *The* * *Triumph of Health and Mirth*, on the Recovery of Lady *Tyrconnel* from a languishing Illness. This

That *I live*, my Lord, is a Proof, that Dependance upon your Lordship and the present Ministry is an Assurance of Success. I am persuaded Distress in many other Instances affects your Soul with a Compassion that always shews itself in a Manner most humane and active, that to forgive Injuries, and confer Benefits, is your Delight, and that to deserve your Friendship is to deserve the Countenance of the best of Men. To be admitted to the Honour of your Lordship's Conversation (permit me to speak but Justice) is to be elegantly introduced into the most instructive as well as entertaining Parts of Literature: It is to be furnished with the finest Observations upon human Nature, and to receive from the most unassuming, sweet, and winning Candour, the worthiest and most polite Maxims—such as are always inforced by the Actions of your own Life.— If my future Morals and Writings should gain any Approbation from Men of Parts and Probity, I must acknowledge all to be the Product of your Lordship's Goodness.—

* *Of the Numbers and Sentiments the following Lines will afford a Specimen.*

> Where *Thames* with Pride beholds *Augusta*'s Charms,
> And either *India* pours into her Arms,—
> High thron'd appears the laughter-loving Dame—
> Goddess of Mirth——
>   O'er the gay World the sweet Inspirer reigns,
> Spleen flies, and Elegance her Pomp sustains;
> Thee, Goddess, thee the fair and young obey,
> Wealth, Wit, and Music, all confess thy Sway.—
>   The Goddess summons each illustrious Name,
> Bids the Gay talk, and forms th' amusive Game,
> She whose fair Throne is fix'd in human Souls,
> From Joy to Joy her Eye delighted rolls:
> But where, she cry'd, is she, my fav'rite she,
> Of all my Race the dearest far to me!

[46] Spring 1730.

Performance is remarkable, not only for the Gayety of the Ideas, and the Melody of the Numbers, but for the agreeable Fiction upon which it is formed.* *Mirth* overwhelmed with Sorrow, for the Sickness of her Favourite, takes a Flight in Quest of her Sister *Health*, whom she finds reclined upon the Brow of a lofty Mountain, amidst the Fragrance of perpetual Spring, with the Breezes of the Morning sporting about her. Being solicited by her Sister *Mirth*, she readily promises her Assistance, flies away in a Cloud, and impregnates the Waters of *Bath* with new Virtues, by which the Sickness of *Belinda* is relieved.

As the Reputation of his Abilities, the particular Circumstances of his Birth and Life, the Splendour of his Appearance, and the Distinction which was for some Time paid him by Lord *Tyrconnel*, intitled him to Familiarity with

> Whose Life's the Source of each refin'd Delight,
> She said, but no *Belinda* glads her Sight—
> In kind low Murmurs all the Loss deplore,
> *Belinda* droops, and Pleasure is no more.
>   The Goddess silent paus'd in museful Air,
> But Mirth like Virtue, cannot long despair.—
> Strait wafted on the tepid Breeze she flies,
> Where *Bath*'s ascending Turrets meet her Eyes.
> She flies, her elder Sister Health to find,
> She finds her on a Mountain's Brow reclin'd,
> Around her Birds in earliest Consort sing,
> Her Cheek the Semblance of the kindling Spring.—
> Loose to the Wind her verdant Vestments flow,
> Her Limbs yet recent from the Springs below:
> Thereof she bathes, then peaceful sits secure,
> Where ev'ry Breath is fragrant, fresh and pure.—
>   Hail, Sister, hail, the kindred Goddess cries,
> No common Suppliant stands before your Eyes—
> Strength, Vigour, Wit, depriv'd of thee decline,
> Each finer Sense that forms Delight is thine—
> Bright Suns by thee diffuse a brighter Blaze,
> And the fresh Green a fresher Green displays—
> Such thy vast Pow'r—The Deity replies,
> Mirth never asks a Boon which Health denies;
> Our mingled Gifts transcend imperial Wealth,
> Health strengthens Mirth, and Mirth inspirits Health.

* See the whole Poem, *Gent. Mag.* Vol. VII. p. 243.

Persons of higher Rank, than those to whose Conversation he had been before admitted, he did not fail to gratify that Curiosity, which induced him to take a nearer View of those whom their Birth, their Employments, or their Fortunes, necessarily place at a Distance from the greatest Part of Mankind, and to examine, whether their Merit was magnified or diminished by the Medium through which it was contemplated; whether the Splendour with which they dazzled their Admirers, was inherent in themselves, or only reflected on them by the Objects that surrounded them; and whether great Men were selected for high Stations, or high Stations made great Men.

For this Purpose, he took all Opportunities of conversing familiarly with those who were most conspicuous at that Time, for their Power, or their Influence; he watched their looser Moments, and examined their domestic Behaviour, with that Acuteness which Nature had given him, and which the uncommon Variety of his Life had contributed to increase, and that Inquisitiveness which must always be produced in a vigorous Mind by an absolute Freedom from all pressing or domestic Engagements. His Discernment was quick, and therefore he soon found in every Person, and in every Affair, something that deserved Attention; he was supported by others, without any Care for himself, and was therefore at Leisure to pursue his Observations.

More Circumstances to constitute a Critic on human Life could not easily concur, nor indeed could any Man who assumed from accidental Advantages more Praise than he could justly claim from his real Merit, admit an Acquaintance more dangerous than that of *Savage*; of whom likewise it must be confessed, that Abilities really exalted above the common Level, or Virtue refined from Passion, or Proof against Corruption could not easily find an abler Judge, or a warmer Advocate.

What was the Result of Mr. *Savage's* Enquiry, though he

was not much accustomed to conceal his Discoveries, it may
not be entirely safe to relate, because the Persons whose
Characters he criticised are powerful; and Power and
Resentment are seldom Strangers; nor would it perhaps be
wholly just, because what he asserted in Conversation might,
though true in general, be heightened by some momentary
Ardour of Imagination, and as it can be delivered only from
Memory, may be imperfectly represented; so that the
Picture at first aggravated, and then unskilfully copied, may
be justly suspected to retain no great Resemblance of the
Original.

It may however be observed, that he did not appear to
have formed very elevated Ideas of those to whom the
Administration of Affairs, or the Conduct of Parties, has
been intrusted; who have been considered as the Advocates
of the Crown, or the Guardians of the People, and who
have obtained the most implicit Confidence, and the loudest
Applauses. Of one particular Person, who has been at one
Time so popular as to be generally esteemed, and at another
so formidable as to be universally detested, he observed, that
his Acquisitions had been small, or that his Capacity was
narrow, and that the whole Range of his Mind was from
Obscenity to Politics, and from Politics to Obscenity.[47]

But the Opportunity of indulging his Speculations on
great Characters was now at an End. He was banished from
the Table of Lord *Tyrconnel*, and turned again adrift upon
the World, without Prospect of finding quickly any other
Harbour. As Prudence was not one of the Virtues by which
he was distinguished, he had made no Provision against a
Misfortune like this. And though it is not to be imagined,
but that the Separation must for some Time have been preceded by Coldness, Peevishness, or Neglect, though it was
undoubtedly the Consequence of accumulated Provocations

---

[47] Walpole, according to G. B. Hill (*Lives of the Poets*, ii. 372, n. 1).
But there is nothing in Johnson's words to point to Walpole in particular.

on both Sides, yet every one that knew *Savage* will readily believe, that to him it was sudden as a Stroke of Thunder; that though he might have transiently suspected it, he had never suffered any Thought so unpleasing to sink into his Mind, but that he had driven it away by Amusements, or Dreams of future Felicity and Affluence, and had never taken any Measures by which he might prevent a Precipitation from Plenty to Indigence.

This Quarrel and Separation, and the Difficulties to which Mr. *Savage* was exposed by them, were soon known both to his Friends and Enemies; nor was it long before he perceived, from the Behaviour of both, how much is added to the Lustre of Genius, by the Ornaments of Wealth.

His Condition did not appear to excite much Compassion; for he had not always been careful to use the Advantages which he enjoyed with that Moderation, which ought to have been with more than usual Caution preserved by him, who knew, if he had reflected, that he was only a Dependant on the Bounty of another, whom he could expect to support him no longer than he endeavoured to preserve his Favour, by complying with his Inclinations, and whom he nevertheless set at Defiance, and was continually irritating by Negligence or Encroachments.

Examples need not be sought at any great Distance to prove that Superiority of Fortune has a natural Tendency to kindle Pride, and that Pride seldom fails to exert itself in Contempt and Insult; and if this is often the Effect of hereditary Wealth, and of Honours enjoyed only by the Merit of others, it is some Extenuation of any indecent Triumphs to which this unhappy Man may have been betrayed, that his Prosperity was heightened by the Force of Novelty, and made more intoxicating by a Sense of the Misery in which he had so long languished, and perhaps of the Insults which he had formerly born, and which he might now think himself entitled to revenge. It is too common for those who have unjustly suffered Pain, to inflict it likewise in their Turn, with the same Injustice, and to imagine that they have a Right to treat others as they have themselves been treated.

That Mr. *Savage* was too much elevated by any good Fortune is generally known; and some Passages of his Introduction to the *Author to be let* sufficiently shew, that he did not wholly refrain from such Satire as he afterwards thought very unjust, when he was exposed to it himself; for when he was afterwards ridiculed in the Character of a distressed Poet, he very easily discovered, that Distress was not a proper Subject for Merriment, or Topic of Invective.[48] He was then able to discern that if Misery be the Effect of Virtue, it ought to reverenced; if of Ill-Fortune, to be pitied; and if of Vice, not to be insulted, because it is perhaps itself a Punishment adequate to the Crime by which it was produced. And the Humanity of that Man can deserve no Panegyric, who is capable of reproaching a Criminal in the Hands of the Executioner.

But these Reflections, though they readily occurred to him in the first and last Parts of his Life, were, I am afraid, for a long Time forgotten; at least they were, like many other Maxims, treasured up in his Mind, rather for Shew than Use, and operated very little upon his Conduct, however elegantly he might sometimes explain, or however forcibly he might inculcate them.

His Degradation therefore from the Condition which he had enjoyed with such wanton Thoughtlessness, was considered by many as an Occasion of Triumph. Those who had before paid their Court to him, without Success, soon returned the Contempt which they had suffered, and they who had received Favours from him, for of such Favours as he could bestow he was very liberal, did not always

[48] Cf. pp. 100–1 and n. 71.

remember them. So much more certain are the Effects of Resentment than of Gratitude: It is not only to many more pleasing to recollect those Faults which place others below them, than those Virtues by which they are themselves comparatively depressed; but it is likewise more easy to neglect, than to recompense; and though there are few who will practise a laborious Virtue, there will never be wanting Multitudes that will indulge an easy Vice.

Savage however was very little disturbed at the Marks of Contempt which his Ill-Fortune brought upon him, from those whom he never esteemed, and with whom he never considered himself as levelled by any Calamities; and though it was not without some Uneasiness, that he saw some, whose Friendship he valued, change their Behaviour; he yet observed their Coldness without much Emotion, considered them as the Slaves of Fortune and the Worshippers of Prosperity; and was more inclined to despise them, than to lament himself.

It does not appear, that after this Return of his Wants, he found Mankind equally favourable to him, as at his first Appearance in the World. His Story, though in Reality not less melancholy, was less affecting, because it was no longer new; it therefore procured him no new Friends, and those that had formerly relieved him thought they might now consign him to others. He was now likewise considered by many rather as criminal, than as unhappy; for the Friends of Lord *Tyrconnel* and of his Mother were sufficiently industrious to publish his Weaknesses, which were indeed very numerous, and nothing was forgotten, that might make him either hateful or ridiculous.

It cannot but be imagined, that such Representations of his Faults must make great Numbers less sensible of his Distress; many who had only an Opportunity to hear one Part, made no Scruple to propagate the Account which they received; many assisted their Circulation from Malice or

Revenge, and perhaps many pretended to credit them, that they might with a better Grace withdraw their Regard, or withhold their Assistance.

Savage however was not one of those, who suffer themselves to be injured without Resistance, nor was less diligent in exposing the Faults of Lord *Tyrconnel*, over whom he obtained at least this Advantage, that he drove him first to the Practice of Outrage and Violence; for he was so much provoked by the Wit and Virulence of *Savage*, that he came with a Number of Attendants, that did no Honour to his Courage, to beat him at a Coffee-House. But it happened that he had left the Place a few Minutes, and his Lordship had without Danger the Pleasure of boasting, how he would have treated him. Mr. *Savage* went next Day to repay his Visit at his own House, but was prevailed on by his Domestics, to retire without insisting upon seeing him.

Lord *Tyrconnel* was accused by Mr. *Savage* of some Actions, which scarcely any Provocations will be thought sufficient to justify; such as seizing what he had in his Lodgings, and other Instances of wanton Cruelty, by which he encreased the Distress of *Savage*, without any Advantage to himself.

These mutual Accusations were retorted on both Sides for many Years,[49] with the utmost Degree of Virulence and Rage, and Time seemed rather to augment than diminish their Resentment; that the Anger of Mr. *Savage* should be kept alive is not strange, because he felt every Day the Consequences of the Quarrel, but it might reasonably have been hoped, that Lord *Tyrconnel* might have relented, and at length have forgot those Provocations, which, however they might have once inflamed him, had not in Reality much hurt him.

---

[49] The quarrel occurred in 1735, just three years before Savage met Johnson and four before Savage left London for ever. Johnson's sense of time is often at fault in the middle section of this biography.

The Spirit of Mr. *Savage* indeed never suffered him to solicite a Reconciliation; he returned Reproach for Reproach, and Insult for Insult; his Superiority of Wit supplied the Disadvantages of his Fortune, and inabled him to form a Party, and prejudice great Numbers in his Favour.

But though this might be some Gratification of his Vanity, it afforded very little Relief to his Necessities, and he was very frequently reduced to uncommon Hardships, of which, however, he never made any mean or importunate Complaints, being formed rather to bear Misery with Fortitude, than enjoy Prosperity with Moderation.

He now thought himself again at Liberty to expose the Cruelty of his Mother, and therefore, I believe, about this Time, published *The Bastard*,[50] a Poem remarkable for the vivacious Sallies of Thought in the Beginning*, where he makes a pompous Enumeration of the imaginary Advantages

* In gayer Hours, when high my Fancy ran,
The Muse, exulting, thus her Lay began.
　Blest be the Bastard's Birth! thro' wondrous Ways,
He shines eccentrick like a Comet's Blaze.
No sickly Fruit of faint Compliance he;
He! stampt in Nature's Mint with Extasy!
He lives to build, not boast, a gen'rous Race:
No tenth Transmitter of a foolish Face.
His daring Hope, no Sire's Example bounds;
His first-born Lights no Prejudice confounds.
He, kindling, from within, requires no Flame,
He glories, in a Bastard's glowing Name.
　—Loos'd to the World's wide Range—enjoin'd no Aim;
Prescrib'd no Duty, and assign'd no Name:
Nature's unbounded Son he stands alone,
His Heart unbiass'd and his Mind his own.
　—— O Mother, yet no Mother!—'tis to you,
My Thanks for such distinguish'd Claims are due.

[50] *The Bastard, a Poem, Inscrib'd with all due reverence to Mrs. Brett, once Countess of Macclesfield.* Published 18 Apr. 1728, seven years before the quarrel with Lord Tyrconnel. Johnson cannot have seen any of the five editions that came out in London in 1728; he used only the reprint in *GM.* 37, 113–14, in which the poem is said to have been first published 'some years ago' and since to have become scarce. Cf. pp. 42–3, 44.

of base Birth, and the pathetic Sentiments at the End, where he recounts the real Calamities which he suffered by the Crime of his Parents.

The Vigour and Spirit of the Verses, the peculiar Circumstances of the Author, the Novelty of the Subject, and the Notoriety of the Story, to which the Allusions are made, procured this Performance a very favourable Reception; great Numbers were immediately dispersed, and Editions were multiplied with unusual Rapidity.

One Circumstance attended the Publication, which *Savage* used to relate with great Satisfaction. His Mother, to whom the Poem was *with due Reverence* inscribed, happened then to be at *Bath*, where she could not conveniently retire from Censure, or conceal herself from Observation; and no sooner did the Reputation of the Poem begin to spread, than she heard it repeated in all Places of Concourse, nor could she enter the Assembly Rooms, or cross the Walks, without being saluted with some Lines from *The Bastard*.

This was perhaps the first Time that ever she discovered

> ——What had I lost, if conjugally kind,
> By Nature hating, yet by Vows confin'd,
> ——You had *faint-drawn* me with a Form alone,
> A lawful Lump of Life by Force your own!
> ——I had been born your dull domestick Heir;
> Load of your Life and Motive of your Care;
> Perhaps been poorly Rich, and meanly Great;
> The Slave of Pomp, a Cypher in the State;
> Lordly neglectful of a Worth unknown,
> And slumb'ring in a *Seat*, by *Chance* my own.
> ——Thus unprophetic, lately uninspir'd,
> I sung; gay, flatt'ring Hope my Fancy fir'd;
> Inly secure, thro' conscious Scorn of Ill;
> Nor taught by Wisdom how to balance Will.
> ——But now expos'd and shrinking from Distress,
> I fly to Shelter while the Tempests press.

After the Mention of the Death of Sinclair, *he goes on thus*:

> ——Where shall my Hope find Rest?—No Mother's Care
> Shielded my infant Innocence with Pray'r:
> No Father's guardian Hand my Youth maintain'd,
> Call'd forth my Virtues, and from Vice restrain'd.

a Sense of Shame, and on this Occasion the Power of Wit was very conspicuous; the Wretch who had, without Scruple, proclaimed herself an Adulteress, and who had first endeavoured to starve her Son, then to transport him, and afterwards to hang him, was not able to bear the Representation of her own Conduct, but fled from Reproach, though she felt no Pain from Guilt, and left *Bath* with the utmost Haste, to shelter herself among the Crouds of *London*.

Thus *Savage* had the Satisfaction of finding, that though he could not reform his Mother, he could punish her, and that he did not always suffer alone.

The Pleasure which he received from this Increase of his poetical Reputation, was sufficient for some Time to over-balance the Miseries of Want, which this Performance did not much alleviate, for it was sold for a very trivial Sum to a Bookseller, who, though the Success was so uncommon, that five Impressions were sold, of which many were undoubtedly very numerous, had not Generosity sufficient to admit the unhappy Writer to any Part of the Profit.

The Sale of this Poem was always mentioned by Mr. *Savage* with the utmost Elevation of Heart, and referred to by him as an incontestable Proof of a general Acknowledgement of his Abilities. It was indeed the only Production of which he could justly boast a general Reception.

But though he did not lose the Opportunity which Success gave him of setting a high Rate on his Abilities, but paid due Deference to the Suffrages of Mankind when they were given in his Favour, he did not suffer his Esteem of himself to depend upon others, nor found anything sacred in the Voice of the People when they were inclined to censure him; he then readily shewed the Folly of expecting that the Publick should judge right, observed how slowly poetical Merit had often forced its Way into the World, he contented himself with the Applause of Men of Judgment; and was somewhat disposed to exclude all those from the Character of Men of Judgment, who did not applaud him.

But he was at other Times more favourable to Mankind, than to think them blind to the Beauties of his Works, and imputed the Slowness of their Sale to other Causes; either they were published at a Time when the Town was empty, or when the Attention of the Publick was engrossed by some Struggle in the Parliament, or some other Object of general Concern; or they were by the Neglect of the Publisher not diligently dispersed, or by his Avarice not advertised with sufficient Frequency. Address, or Industry, or Liberality, was always wanting; and the Blame was laid rather on any other Person than the Author.

By Arts like these, Arts which every Man practises in some Degree, and to which too much of the little Tranquillity of Life is to be ascribed, *Savage* was always able to live at Peace with himself. Had he indeed only made use of these Expedients to alleviate the Loss or Want of Fortune or Reputation, or any other Advantage, which it is not in Man's Power to bestow upon himself, they might have been justly mentioned as Instances of a philosophical Mind, and very properly proposed to the Imitation of Multitudes, who, for want of diverting their Imaginations with the same Dexterity, languish under Afflictions which might be easily removed.

It were doubtless to be wished, that Truth and Reason were universally prevalent; that every thing were esteemed according to its real Value; and that Men would secure themselves from being disappointed in their Endeavours after Happiness, by placing it only in Virtue, which is always to be obtained; but if adventitious and foreign Pleasures must be persued, it would be perhaps of some Benefit, since that Persuit must frequently be fruitless, if the Practice of *Savage* could be taught, that Folly might be an Antidote to Folly, and one Fallacy be obviated by another.

But the Danger of this pleasing Intoxication must not be concealed; nor indeed can any one, after having observed the Life of *Savage*, need to be cautioned against it. By imputing none of his Miseries to himself, he continued to act upon the same Principles, and follow the same Path; was never made wiser by his Sufferings, nor preserved by one Misfortune from falling into another. He proceeded throughout his Life to tread the same Steps on the same Circle; always applauding his past Conduct, or at least forgetting it, to amuse himself with Phantoms of Happiness, which were dancing before him; and willingly turned his Eyes from the Light of Reason, when it would have discovered the Illusion, and shewn him, what he never wished to see, his real State.

He is even accused, after having lulled his Imagination with those ideal Opiates, of having tried the same Experiment upon his Conscience; and having accustomed himself to impute all Deviations from the right to foreign Causes, it is certain that he was upon every Occasion too easily reconciled to himself, and that he appeared very little to regret those Practices which had impaired his Reputation. The reigning Error of his Life was, that he mistook the Love for the Practice of Virtue, and was indeed not so much a good Man, as the Friend of Goodness.

This at least must be allowed him, that he always preserved a strong Sense of the Dignity, the Beauty and the Necessity of Virtue, and that he never contributed deliberately to spread Corruption amongst Mankind; his Actions, which were generally precipitate, were often blameable, but his Writings being the Productions of Study, uniformly tended to the Exaltation of the Mind, and the Propagation of Morality and Piety.

These Writings may improve Mankind, when his Failings

shall be forgotten, and therefore he must be considered upon the whole as a Benefactor to the World; nor can his personal Example do any hurt, since whoever hears of his Faults, will hear of the Miseries which they brought upon him, and which would deserve less Pity, had not his Condition been such as made his Faults pardonable. He may be considered as a Child *exposed* to all the Temptations of Indigence, at an Age when Resolution was not yet strengthened by Conviction, nor Virtue confirmed by Habit; a Circumstance which in his *Bastard* he laments in a very affecting Manner.

——No Mother's Care
Shielded my Infant Innocence with Prayer:
No Father's guardian Hand my Youth maintain'd,
Call'd forth my Virtues, and from Vice restrain'd.

The *Bastard*, however it might provoke or mortify his Mother, could not be expected to melt her to Compassion, so that he was still under the same Want of the Necessaries of Life, and he therefore exerted all the Interest, which his Wit, or his Birth, or his Misfortunes could procure, to obtain upon the Death of *Eusden*[51] the Place of Poet Laureat, and prosecuted his Application with so much Diligence, that the King publickly declared it his Intention to bestow it upon him; but such was the Fate of *Savage*, that even the King, when he intended his Advantage, was disappointed in his Schemes; for the Lord Chamberlain, who has the Disposal of the Laurel as one of the Appendages of his Office, either did not know the King's Design, or did not approve it, or thought the Nomination of the Laureat an Encroachment upon his Rights, and therefore bestowed the Laurel upon *Colly Cibber*.

Mr. *Savage* thus disappointed took a Resolution of applying to the Queen, that having once given him Life, she

[51] Laurence Eusden died on 27 September 1730 and Colley Cibber was made Poet Laureat on 3 Dec., five years before Savage's quarrel with Lord Tyrconnel.

would enable him to support it, and therefore published a short Poem on her Birth-Day, to which he gave the odd Title of *Volunteer Laureat*.[52] The Event of this Essay he has himself related in the following Letter, which he prefixed to the Poem, when he afterwards reprinted it in the *Gentleman's Magazine*, from whence I have copied it intire, as this was one of the few Attempts in which Mr. *Savage* succeeded.

Mr. *Urban*,

In your Magazine for *February* you published the last *Volunteer Laureat*, written on a very melancholy Occasion, viz. the Death of the Royal Patroness of Arts and Literature in general, and of the Author of that Poem in particular; I now send you the first that Mr. *Savage* wrote under that Title.———This Gentleman, notwithstanding a very considerable Interest, being, on the Death of Mr. *Eusden*, disappointed of the Laureat's Place, wrote the following Verses; which were no sooner published, but the late Queen sent to a Bookseller for them: The Author had not at that Time a Friend either to get him introduced, or his Poem presented at Court; yet such was the unspeakable Goodness of that Princess, that, notwithstanding this Act of Ceremony was wanting, in a few Days after Publication, Mr. *Savage* received a Bank-Bill of fifty Pounds,[53] and a gracious Message from her Majesty, by the Lord *North* and *Guilford*, to this Effect: 'That her Majesty was highly pleased with the Verses; that she took particularly kind his Lines there relating to the King; that he had Permission to write annually on the

[52] Queen Caroline's birthday was 1 Mar., and each annual number of Savage's *Volunteer Laureat* came out punctually on that day. No. 1 was published in 1732, and republished on the Queen's death in *GM*. 38. 210 along with the explanatory letter that Johnson has reprinted, which had been signed 'T.B.' (=Thomas Birch). Johnson omitted the initials, thinking Savage to have been the author. The text of the poem was omitted in 75, 77b, and all later editions during Johnson's lifetime. Minor revisions were made in the letter when the poem was cut, but without it the words written immediately afterwards ('Such was the Performance') are meaningless. Cf. p. 127 and n.

[53] The payment of this, or of a like amount the following year, is recorded in an account book in the Royal Archives at Windsor Castle.

same Subject; and that he should yearly receive the like Present, till something better (which was her Majesty's Intention) could be done for him.' After this he was permitted to present one of his annual Poems to her Majesty, had the Honour of kissing her Hand, and met with the most gracious Reception.

Your's, &c.

The VOLUNTEER LAUREAT.

A POEM: On the *Queen's Birth-Day*. Humbly addressed to her MAJESTY.

Twice twenty tedious Moons have roll'd away,
Since Hope, kind Flatt'rer! tun'd my pensive Lay,[54]
Whisp'ring , that you, who rais'd me from Despair,
Meant, by your Smiles, to make Life worth my Care;
With pitying Hand an Orphan's Tears to screen,
And o'er the motherless extend the Queen.
'Twill be—the Prophet guides the Poet's Strain!
Grief never touch'd a Heart like your's in vain:
Heav'n gave you Power, because you love to bless,
And pity, when you feel it, is Redress.
    Two Fathers join'd to rob my Claim of one!
My Mother too thought fit to have no Son!
The Senate next, whose Aid the helpless own,
Forgot my Infant Wrongs, and mine alone!
Yet Parents pitiless, nor Peers unkind,
Nor Titles lost, nor Woes mysterious join'd,
Strip me of Hope—by Heav'n thus lowly laid,
To find a *Pharoah*'s Daughter in the Shade.
    You cannot hear unmov'd, when Wrongs implore,
Your Heart is Woman, though your Mind be more;
Kind, like the Pow'r who gave you to our Pray'rs,
You would not lengthen Life to sharpen Cares:

[54] It was rather more than four years since Savage had been saved from the gallows by a royal pardon and (so he supposed) promised financial assistance. The 'pensive Lay' was the *Bastard*, in the concluding lines of which he had hinted at his hope of being adopted by the Queen and so acquiring a royal mother in place of the natural one who had abandoned him.

They who a barren Leave to live bestow,
Snatch but from Death to sacrifice to Woe.
Hated by her, from whom my Life I drew,
Whence should I hope, if not from Heav'n and you?
Nor dare I groan beneath Affliction's Rod,
My Queen, my Mother; and my Father, God.

The pitying Muses saw me Wit pursue,
A *Bastard Son*, alas! on that Side too,
Did not your Eyes exalt the Poet's Fire,
And what the Muse denies, the Queen inspire;
While rising thus your heavenly Soul to view,
I learn, how Angels think, by copying you.

Great Princess! 'tis decreed—once ev'ry Year
I march uncall'd your Laureat Volunteer;
Thus shall your Poet his low Genius raise,
And charm the World with Truths too vast for Praise.
Nor need I dwell on Glories all your own,
Since surer Means to tempt your Smiles are known;
Your Poet shall allot your Lord his Part,
And paint him in his noblest Throne, your Heart.

Is there a Greatness that adorns him best,
A rising Wish that ripens in his Breast?
Has he fore-meant some distant Age to bless,
Disarm Oppression, or expel Distress?
Plans he some Scheme to reconcile Mankind,
People the Seas, and busy ev'ry Wind?
Would he, by Pity, the deceiv'd reclaim,
And smile contending Factions into Shame?
Would his Example lend his Laws a Weight,
And breathe his own soft Morals o'er his State?
The Muse shall find it all, shall make it seen,
And teach the World his Praise, to charm his Queen.

Such be the annual Truths my Verse imparts,
Nor frown, fair *Fav'rite* of a People's Hearts!
Happy if plac'd, perchance, beneath your Eye,
My Muse unpension'd might her Pinions try,
Fearless to fail, whilst you indulge your Flame,
And bid me proudly boast your Laureat's Name;

Renobled thus by Wreaths my Queen bestows,
I lose all Memory of Wrongs and Woes.

Such was the Performance, and such its Reception; a
Reception which, though by no Means unkind, was yet not
in the highest Degree generous: To chain down the Genius
of a Writer to an annual Panegyric, shewed in the Queen
too much Desire of hearing her own Praises, and a greater
Regard to herself than to him on whom her Bounty was
conferred. It was a kind of avaricious Generosity, by which
Flattery was rather purchased than Genius rewarded.

Mrs. *Oldfield* had formerly given him the same Allowance with much more heroic Intention; she had no other
View than to enable him to prosecute his Studies, and to
set himself above the Want of Assistance, and was contented
with doing good without stipulating for Encomiums.

Mr. *Savage* however was not at Liberty to make Excep-
tions, but was ravished with the Favours which he had
received, and probably yet more with those which he was
promised; he considered himself now as a Favourite of the
Queen, and did not doubt but a few annual Poems would
establish him in some profitable Employment.

He therefore assumed the Title of *Volunteer Laureat*, not
without some Reprehensions from *Cibber*, who informed
him, that the Title of *Laureat* was a Mark of Honour conferred by the King, from whom all Honour is derived, and
which therefore no Man has a Right to bestow upon himself; and added, that he might with equal Propriety stile
himself a Volunteer Lord, or Volunteer Baronet. It cannot
be denied that the Remark was just, but *Savage* did not
think any Title, which was conferred upon Mr. *Cibber*, so
honourable as that the Usurpation of it could be imputed
to him as an Instance of very exorbitant Vanity, and therefore continued to write under the same Title, and received
every Year the same Reward.

He did not appear to consider these Encomiums as Tests of his Abilities, or as any thing more than annual Hints to the Queen of her Promise, or Acts of Ceremony, by the Performance of which he was intitled to his Pension, and therefore did not labour them with great Diligence, or print more than fifty each Year, except that for some of the last Years he regularly inserted them in the *Gentleman's Magazine*, by which they were dispersed over the Kingdom.[55]

Of some of them he had himself so low an Opinion, that he intended to omit them in the Collection of Poems, for which he printed Proposals, and solicited Subscriptions;[56] nor can it seem strange, that being confined to the same Subject, he should be at some times indolent, and at others unsuccessful, that he should sometimes delay a disagreeable Task, till it was too late to perform it well; or that he should sometimes repeat the same Sentiment on the same Occasion, or at others be misled by an Attempt after Novelty to forced Conceptions, and far-fetched Images.

He wrote indeed with a double Intention, which supplied him with some Variety, for his Business was to praise the Queen for the Favours which he had received, and to complain to her of the Delay of those which she had promised: In some of his Pieces, therefore, Gratitude is predominant, and in some Discontent; in some he represents himself as happy in her Patronage, and in others as disconsolate to find himself neglected.

Her Promise, like other Promises made to this unfortunate Man, was never performed, though he took sufficient Care that it should not be forgotten. The Publication of his

---

[55] In 1775 Evans was able to print only four of the seven in his edition of Savage's *Works*, and two more in the second edition in 1777. The missing one, no. 3, has never been recovered.

[56] Johnson is vague about Savage's project of a subscription edition of his works, which never materialized. No copy of any separate proposals has come to light, though in 1734 he arranged for the printing of a batch of them (Sloane MS. 4318, ff. 41, 53). In 1737 a proposal was, however, published as an advertisement in the *Gentleman's Magazine*. Cf. p. 111.

Volunteer Laureat procured him no other Reward than a regular Remittance of fifty Pounds.

He was not so depressed by his Disappointments as to neglect any Opportunity that was offered of advancing his Interest. When the Princess *Anne* was married, he wrote a Poem upon her Departure,[57] only, as he declared, *because it was expected from him,* and he was not willing to bar his own Prospects by any Appearance of Neglect.

He never mentioned any Advantage gain'd by this Poem, or any Regard that was paid to it, and therefore it is likely that it was considered at Court as an Act of Duty to which he was obliged by his Dependence, and which it was therefore not necessary to reward by any new Favour: Or perhaps the Queen really intended his Advancement, and therefore thought it superfluous to lavish Presents upon a Man whom she intended to establish for Life.

About this Time not only his Hopes were in Danger of being frustrated, but his Pension likewise of being obstructed by an accidental Calumny. The Writer of the *Daily Courant,* a Paper then published under the Direction of the Ministry, charged him with a Crime, which though not very great in itself, would have been remarkably invidious in him, and might very justly have incensed the Queen against him. He was accused by Name of influencing Elections against the Court, by appearing at the Head of a Tory Mob; nor did the Accuser fail to aggravate his Crime, by representing it as the Effect of the most atrocious Ingratitude, and a kind of Rebellion against the Queen, who had first preserved him from an infamous Death, and afterwards distinguished him by her Favour, and supported him by her Charity. The Charge, as it was open and confident, was likewise by good Fortune very particular. The Place of the Transaction was mentioned, and the whole Series of

[57] *On the Departure of the Prince and Princess of Orange,* published July 1734; republished as the 'Genius of Liberty', *GM.* 38. 315.

the Rioter's Conduct related. This Exactness made Mr. *Savage*'s Vindication easy, for he never had in his Life seen the Place which was declared to be the Scene of his Wickedness, nor ever had been present in any Town when its Representatives were chosen. This Answer he therefore made haste to publish, with all the Circumstances necessary to make it credible, and very reasonably demanded, that the Accusation should be retracted in the same Paper, that he might no longer suffer the Imputation of Sedition and Ingratitude. This Demand was likewise pressed by him in a private Letter to the Author of the Paper, who either trusting to the Protection of those whose Defence he had undertaken, or having entertained some personal Malice against Mr. *Savage*, or fearing lest, by retracting so confident an Assertion, he should impair the Credit of his Paper, refused to give him that Satisfaction.

Mr. *Savage* therefore thought it necessary, to his own Vindication, to prosecute him in the King's Bench; but as he did not find any ill Effects from the Accusation, having sufficiently cleared his Innocence, he thought any farther Procedure would have the Appearance of Revenge, and therefore willingly dropped it.[58]

He saw soon afterwards a Process commenced in the same

---

[58] The principal essay in the *Daily Courant* for 2 May 1735 was an attack on Savage's recently published *Progress of a Divine* on account of its abuse of the clergy: 'And surely it cannot be *Wisdom*, I think, for one, who has just escap'd Hanging, to banter others upon *reading their Neck-Verse, v.* 14. Or to talk of *supporting Country Mobs, v.* 329, when there is an Information now depending in the Court of King's Bench against him for a *Riot* at a late election in *Flintshire*. . . . And very ungrateful is it, thus to traduce a most *worthy Prelate* [the Bishop of London], whom the King is pleased to Countenance; much more to fling Dirt upon the very Throne, from whence he so lately received the greatest of all Favours, even Life itself.' This accusation was due to a confusion of identities. In the archives of the Court of King's Bench in the Public Record Office is mention of the trial of a 'Richard Surridge late of the burrough of Flint in the said county of Flint, Esq. otherwise called Richard Savage' for 'certain trespasses contempts riots routs unlawful assemblies assaults false imprisonments and misdemeanours' committed

Court against himself, on an Information in which he was accused of writing and publishing an obscene Pamphlet.

It was always Mr. *Savage*'s Desire to be distinguished, and when any Controversy became popular, he never wanted some Reason for engaging in it with Ardour, and appearing at the Head of the Party which he had chosen. As he was never celebrated for his Prudence, he had no sooner taken his Side, and informed himself of the chief Topics of the Dispute, than he took all Opportunities of asserting and propagating his Principles, without much Regard to his own Interest, or any other visible Design than that of drawing upon himself the Attention of Mankind.

The Dispute between the Bishop of *London* and the Chancellor is well known to have been for some Time the chief Topic of political Conversation, and therefore Mr. *Savage*, in Pursuance of his Character, endeavoured to become conspicuous among the Controvertists with which every Coffee-House was filled on that Occasion. He was an indefatigable Opposer of all the Claims of Ecclesiastical Power, though he did not know on what they were founded, and was therefore no Friend to the Bishop of *London*. But he had another Reason for appearing as a warm Advocate for Dr. *Rundle*, for he was the Friend of Mr. *Foster* and Mr. *Thompson*, who were the Friends of Mr. *Savage*.

Thus remote was his Interest in the Question, which however, as he imagined, concerned him so nearly, that it was not sufficient to harangue and dispute, but necessary likewise to write upon it.

He therefore engaged with great Ardour in a new Poem, called by him, *The Progress of a Divine*, in which he conducts a profligate Priest by all the Gradations of

at Oswestry in Shropshire (Easter term, 8 Geo. II). This Richard Surridge or Savage was acquitted. The election in question was that of May 1734. The answer that Savage is said to have published has not come to light, nor is there any record of a prosecution of the newspaper in the files of the court.

Wickedness from a poor Curacy in the Country, to the highest Preferments of the Church, and describes with that Humour which was natural to him, and that Knowledge which was extended to all the Diversities of human Life, his Behaviour in every Station, and insinuates, that this Priest thus accomplished found at last a Patron in the Bishop of *London*.[59]

When he was asked by one of his Friends, on what Pretence he could charge the Bishop with such an Action, he had no more to say, than that he had only inverted the Accusation, and that he thought it reasonable to believe, that he, who obstructed the Rise of a good Man without Reason, would for bad Reasons promote the Exaltation of a Villain.

The Clergy were universally provoked by this Satire, and *Savage*, who, as was his constant Practice, had set his Name to his Performance, was censured in the *Weekly Miscellany** with a Severity, which he did not seem inclined to forget.[60]

---

* *A short Satire was likewise published in the same Paper, in which were the following Lines:*

> For cruel Murder doom'd to Hempen Death,
> *Savage*, by royal Grace, prolong'd his Breath.
> Well might you think, he spent his *future* Years
> In Prayer, and Fasting and repentant Tears.

---

[59] The dispute between the Bishop of London, Edmund Gibson, and the Lord Chancellor, Charles Talbot, was over the proposed elevation of Thomas Rundle to the see of Gloucester. Rundle was Low Church and a friend of the popular dissenter, James Foster. Savage was on intimate terms with both Rundle and Foster. *The Progress of a Divine*, however, has little bearing on that dispute, and seems more likely to have been inspired by a charge, recently made in public, that Gibson had unjustly procured the acquittal of a clergyman accused of unnatural vice (*GM*. 34, 153). Later Johnson remarked that Savage had determined never to reprint this poem, and it was excluded from the *Works of the English Poets* (1779).

[60] *Weekly Miscellany*, no. 121 (5 Apr. 1735); copied by both the *Gentleman's Magazine* and the *London Magazine*. The reply, defending 'that ingenious gentleman R: Savage. Esq.', came in the May number of the *Gentleman's Magazine*, written by 'a *Wiltshire* Correspondent'.

But a Return of Invective was not thought a sufficient Punishment. The Court of *King's Bench* was therefore moved against him, and he was obliged to return an Answer to a Charge of Obscenity. It was urged in his Defence, that Obscenity was criminal when it was intended to promote the Practice of Vice, but that Mr. *Savage* had only introduced obscene Ideas with the View of exposing them to

> —But, O vain Hope!——the truly *Savage* cries,
> 'Priests, and their slavish Doctrines, I despise.
> Shall I————————
> Who, by free Thinking to free Action fir'd,
> In midnight Brawls a deathless Name acquir'd,
> Now stoop to *learn* of *Ecclesiastic Men?*——
> ——No arm'd with Rhime, at Priests I'll take my Aim,
> Though Prudence bids me murder but their Fame.'
> *Weekly Miscellany.*

An Answer was published in the Gentleman's *Magazine, written by an unknown Hand, from which the following Lines are selected*:

> Transform'd by thoughtless Rage, and midnight Wine,
> From Malice free, and push'd without *Design*;
> In equal Brawl if *Savage* lung'd a Thrust,
> And brought the Youth a Victim to the Dust:
> So strong the Hand of Accident appears,
> The royal Hand from Guilt and Vengeance clears.
>   Instead of wasting '*all thy future Years,*
> *Savage in Pray'r and vain repentant Tears,*'
> Exert thy Pen to mend a vicious Age,
> To curb the Priest, and sink his High-Church Rage;
> To shew what Frauds the holy Vestments hide,
> The Nests of Av'rice, Lust, and pedant Pride.
> Then change the Scene, let Merit brightly shine,
> And round the Patriot twist the Wreath divine;
> The heav'nly Guide deliver down to Fame;
> In well-tun'd Lays transmit a *Foster*'s Name.
> Touch every Passion with harmonious Art,
> Exalt the Genius, and correct the Heart.
> Thus future Times shall royal Grace extol;
> Thus polish'd Lines thy present Fame enrol.
> ——But grant————
> ——Maliciously that *Savage* plung'd the *Steel*,
> And made the Youth its shining Vengeance feel;
> My Soul abhors the Act, the Man detests,
> But more the Bigotry in priestly Breasts.
> *Gentleman's Magazine*, May 1735.

Detestation, and of amending the Age by shewing the Deformity of Wickedness. This Plea was admitted, and Sir *Philip Yorke*, who then presided in that Court, dismissed the Information with Encomiums upon the Purity and Excellence of Mr. *Savage*'s Writings.[61]

The Prosecution however answered in some Measure the Purpose of those by whom it was set on Foot, for Mr. *Savage* was so far intimidated by it, that when the Edition of his Poem was sold, he did not venture to reprint it, so that it was in a short Time forgotten, or forgotten by all but those whom it offended.

It is said, that some Endeavours were used to incense the Queen against him, but he found Advocates to obviate at least Part of their Effect; for though he was never advanced, he still continued to receive his Pension.

This Poem drew more Infamy upon him than any incident of his Life, and as his Conduct cannot be vindicated, it is proper to secure his Memory from Reproach, by informing those whom he made his Enemies, that he never intended to repeat the Provocation; and that, though whenever he thought he had any Reason to complain of the Clergy, he used to threaten them with a new Edition of *The Progress of a Divine*, it was his calm and settled Resolution to suppress it for ever.

He once intended to have made a better Reparation for the Folly or Injustice with which he might be charged, by writing another Poem, called, *The Progress of a Free-Thinker*, whom he intended to lead through all the Stages of Vice and Folly, to convert him from Virtue to Wickedness, and from Religion to Infidelity by all the modish Sophistry used for that Purpose; and at last to dismiss him by his own Hand into the other World.

---

[61] No trace of this trial can be found in the records of the Court of King's Bench among either civil or criminal cases during Easter or Trinity terms 1735.

That he did not execute this Design is a real Loss to Mankind, for he was too well acquainted with all the Scenes of Debauchery to have failed in his Representations of them, and too zealous for Virtue not to have represented them in such a Manner as should expose them either to Ridicule or Detestation.

But this Plan was like others, formed and laid aside, till the Vigour of his Imagination was spent, and the Effervescence of Invention had subsided, but soon gave Way to some other Design which pleased by its Novelty for a while, and then was neglected like the former.

He was still in his usual Exigencies, having no certain Support but the Pension allowed him by the Queen, which though it might have kept an exact Oeconomist from Want, was very far from being sufficient for Mr. *Savage*, who had never been accustomed to dismiss any of his Appetites without the Gratification which they solicited, and whom nothing but Want of Money withheld from partaking of every Pleasure that fell within his View.

His Conduct with regard to his Pension was very particular.[62] No sooner had he changed the Bill, than he vanished from the Sight of all his Acquaintances, and lay for some Time out of the Reach of all the Enquiries that Friendship or Curiosity could make after him; at length he appeared again pennyless as before, but never informed even those whom he seemed to regard most, where he had been, nor was his Retreat ever discovered.

This was his constant Practice during the whole Time that he received the Pension from the Queen: He regularly disappeared and returned. He indeed affirmed, that he retired to study, and that the Money supported him in Solitude for many Months; but his Friends declared, that the short Time

---

[62] In his *Dictionary* Johnson gave six senses of this word, of which the last was 'odd'. 'This', he added, 'is commonly used in a sense of contempt.'

in which it was spent sufficiently confuted his own Account of his Conduct.

His Politeness and his Wit still raised him Friends, who were desirous of setting him at length free from that Indigence by which he had been hitherto oppressed, and therefore solicited Sir *Robert Walpole* in his Favour with so much Earnestness, that they obtained a Promise of the next Place that should become vacant, not exceeding two hundred Pounds a Year. This Promise was made with an uncommon Declaration, *that it was not the Promise of a Minister to a Petitioner, but of a Friend to his Friend.*

Mr. *Savage* now concluded himself set at Ease for ever, and as he observes in a Poem* written on that Incident of

* *The Poet's Dependence on a Statesman, which was published in the* Gentleman's Magazine (Vol. VI, p. 225) *and contained among others the following Passages.*

> Some seem to hint, and others Proof will bring,
> That, from Neglect, my num'rous Hardships spring.
> 'Seek the *great Man,*' they cry——'tis then decreed,
> In *him* if I court *Fortune,* I succeed.
> What Friends to second? Who, for *me,* should sue,
> Have Int'rests, partial to *themselves,* in View.
> They own my matchless Fate Compassion draws,
> They all wish well, lament, but drop my Cause.
> ——Say, shall I turn where *Lucre* points my Views;
> At first desert my Friends, at length abuse?
> But, on less Terms, in *Promise* he complies;
> Years bury Years, and Hopes on Hopes arise;
> I trust, am trusted on my fairy Gain;
> And Woes on Woes attend an endless Train.
> Be Posts dispos'd at Will!——I have, for these,
> No Gold to plead, no Impudence to teaze.
> All secret Service from my Soul I hate;
> All dark Intrigues of Pleasure, or of State.
> ——Where these are not what Claim to me belongs;
> Though mine the *Muse* and *Virtue, Birth* and *Wrongs?*
> Where lives the *Statesman,* so in *Honour* clear,
> To give where he has nought to hope, nor fear?
> No!—there to seek, is but to find fresh Pain:
> The Promise broke, renew'd and broke again;
> To be, as Humour deigns, receiv'd, refus'd;
> By turns affronted, and by turns amus'd;
> To lose that Time, which worthier Thoughts require;
> To lose that Health, which should those Thoughts inspire;

his Life,[63] *trusted* and *was trusted*, but soon found that his Confidence was ill-grounded, and this *friendly* Promise was not inviolable. He spent a long Time in Solicitations, and at last despaired and desisted.

He did not indeed deny that he had given the Minister some Reason to believe that he should not strengthen his own Interest by advancing him, for he had taken Care to distinguish himself in Coffee-Houses as an Advocate for the Ministry of the last Years of Queen *Anne,* and was always ready to justify the Conduct, and exalt the Character of Lord *Bolingbroke,* whom he mentions with great Regard in an Epistle upon Authors, which he wrote about that Time, but was too wise to publish, and of which only some Fragments* have appeared, inserted by him in the Magazine after his Retirement.[64]

> To starve on Hope; or, like Camelions, fare
> On *ministerial Faith,* which means but Air.
> —A Scene *will* shew—(all-righteous Vision haste)
> The Meek exalted, and the Proud debas'd!——
> Oh! to be there!—to tread that friendly Shore;
> Where *Falsehood, Pride* and *Statesmen* are no more?

* *From these the following Lines are selected as an Instance rather of his Impartiality than Genius.*

> Materials which Belief in Gazettes claim,
> Loose strung, run gingling into Hist'ry's Name.

---

[63] Published 1736.

[64] The ministry of the last years of Queen Anne was the Oxford–Bolingbroke one that fell in 1714 on the Queen's death and was later accused of having had active Jacobite sympathies. By 1735 this would have been a politically dead issue if Bolingbroke had not become in the interval the political philosopher of the opposition to Walpole and George II. Savage, who received a pension regularly from the Queen, was playing a dangerous and ungrateful game in publicly supporting the Opposition, and so Johnson is justifiably sharp in his language; cf. pp. 81–2 and n. Savage's 'Epistles upon Authors' were probably completed in 1738 or 1739, for he sent the manuscript of them to Thomas Birch for transmission to the *Gentleman's Magazine* in an undated letter that was most likely written between 1 Sept. 1738 and July 1739 (Sloane MS. 4318, f. 49). They were never published, except for the part entitled 'On false Historians' which concluded with a panegyric on Lord Bolingbroke (*GM.* 41. 491).

To despair was not, however, the Character of *Savage*, when one Patronage failed, he had recourse to another. The Prince was now extremely popular, and had very

Thick as Egyptian Clouds of raining Flies;
As thick as Worms where Man corrupting lies;
As Pests obscene that haunt the ruin'd Pile;
As Monsters flound'ring in the muddy Nile;
Minutes, Memoirs, Views and Reviews appear,
Where Slander darkens each recorded Year.
In a past Reign is feign'd some am'rous League;
Some Ring, or Letter, now reveals the' Intrigue;
Queens with their Minions work unseemly Things,
And Boys grow Dukes, when Catamites to Kings!
Does a Prince die? What Poisons they surmise?
No Royal Mortal sure by Nature dies.
Is a Prince born? What Birth more base believ'd?
Or, what's more strange, his Mother ne'er conceiv'd!
Thus Slander popular o'er Truth prevails,
And easy Minds imbibe romantic Tales.
    Some usurp Names——an *English Garreteer*,
From *Minutes* forg'd, is *Monsieur Menager*.
    ——Where *hear-say Knowledge* sits on public Names,
And bold *Conjecture* or extols, or blames,
Spring *Party Libels*; from whose Ashes dead,
A *Monster*, misnam'd *Hist'ry*, lifts its Head.
Contending Factions croud to hear it's Roar!
But when once heard, it dies to noise no more.
From these no Answer, no Applause from those,
O'er half they simper, and o'er half they doze.
So when in Senate, with egregious Pate,
Perks up, Sir——in some deep Debate;
He hems, looks wise, tunes thin his lab'ring Throat,
To prove Black White, postpone or palm the Vote;
In sly Contempt, some, *hear him! hear him!* cry;
Some yawn, some sneer; none second, none reply.
    But dare such Miscreants now rush abroad,
By Blanket, Cane, Pump, Pillory, unaw'd?
Dare they imp Falshood thus, and plume her Wings,
From present Characters, and recent Things?
Yes, what Untruths? Or Truths in what Disguise?
What *Boyers*, and what *Oldmixons* arise?
What *Facts* from all but *them* and *Slander* screen'd?
Here meets a *Council*, no where else conven'd.
There, from *Originals*, come, thick as spawn,
Letters ne'er wrote, Memorials never drawn;
To *secret Conf'rence*, never held, they yoke
Treaties ne'er plann'd, and Speeches never spoke.
From, *Oldmixon*, thy Brow, too well we know,
Like *Sin* from *Satan's*, far and wide they go.

liberally rewarded the Merit of some Writers whom Mr. *Savage* did not think superior to himself, and therefore he resolved to address a Poem to him.

For this Purpose he made Choice of a Subject, which could regard only Persons of the highest Rank and greatest Affluence, and which was therefore proper for a Poem intended to procure the Patronage of a Prince; and having retired for some Time to *Richmond*, that he might prosecute his Design in full Tranquillity, without the Temptations of Pleasure, or the Solicitations of Creditors, by which his Meditations were in equal Danger of being disconcerted, he produced *a Poem On public Spirit, with regard to public Works.*[65]

The Plan of this Poem is very extensive, and comprises a Multitude of Topics, each of which might furnish Matter sufficient for a long Performance, and of which some have already employed more eminent Writers; but as he was perhaps not fully acquainted with the whole Extent of his own Design, and was writing to obtain a Supply of Wants too pressing to admit of long or accurate Enquiries, he passes negligently over many public Works, which, even in his own Opinion, deserved to be more elaborately treated.

But though he may sometimes disappoint his Reader by transient Touches upon these Subjects, which have often

> In vain may *St. John* safe in Conscience sit,
> In vain with Truth confute, contemn with Wit:
> Confute, contemn, amid selected Friends;
> There sinks the Justice, there the Satire ends.
> Here though a *Cent'ry* scarce such Leaves unclose,
> From Mold and Dust the Slander sacred grows.
> Now none reply where all despise the Page;
> But will dumb Scorn deceive no future Age?
> *Gentleman's Magazine*, Sept. 1741.

---

[65] The first version of this poem, which seems to have been unknown to Johnson, was published in 1736 with the title *A Poem on the Birthday of the Prince of Wales,* and was a failure. Savage rewrote and enlarged it, publishing it again in 1737 with the title *Of Public Spirit in Regard to Public Works.* A second edition came out in 1739 containing the lines quoted on p. 94.

been considered, and therefore naturally raise Expectations, he must be allowed amply to compensate his Omissions by expatiating in the Conclusion of his Work upon a Kind of Beneficence not yet celebrated by any eminent Poet, though it now appears more susceptible of Embellishments, more adapted to exalt the Ideas, and affect the Passions, than many of those which have hitherto been thought most worthy of the Ornaments of Verse. The Settlement of Colonies in uninhabited Countries, the Establishment of those in Security whose Misfortunes have made their own Country no longer pleasing or safe, the Acquisition of Property without Injury to any, the Appropriation of the waste and luxuriant Bounties of Nature, and the Enjoyment of those Gifts which Heaven has scattered upon Regions uncultivated and unoccupied, cannot be considered without giving Rise to a great Number of pleasing Ideas, and bewildering the Imagination in delightful Prospects; and, therefore, whatever Speculations they may produce in those who have confined themselves to political Studies, naturally fixed the Attention, and excited the Applause of a Poet. The Politician, when he considers Men driven into other Countries for Shelter, and obliged to retire to Forests and Deserts, and pass their Lives and fix their Posterity in the remotest Corners of the World, to avoid those Hardships which they suffer or fear in their native Place, may very properly enquire why the Legislature does not provide a Remedy for these Miseries, rather than encourage an Escape from them. He may conclude, that the Flight of every honest Man is a Loss to the Community, that those who are unhappy without Guilt ought to be relieved, and the Life which is overburthened by accidental Calamities, set at Ease by the Care of the Publick, and that those, who have by Misconduct forfeited their Claim to Favour, ought rather to be made useful to the Society which they have injured, than be driven from it. But the Poet is employed in a more pleasing Undertaking than that of proposing Laws, which, however just or expedient, will never be made, or endeavouring to reduce to rational Schemes of Government Societies which were formed by Chance, and are conducted by the private Passions of those who preside in them. He guides the unhappy Fugitive from Want and Persecution, to Plenty, Quiet, and Security, and seats him in Scenes of peaceful Solitude, and undisturbed Repose.

Savage has not forgotten amidst the pleasing Sentiments which this Prospect of Retirement suggested to him to censure those Crimes which have been generally committed by the Discoverers of new Regions, and to expose the enormous Wickedness of making War upon barbarous Nations because they cannot resist, and of invading Countries because they are fruitful; of extending Navigation only to propagate Vice, and of visiting distant Lands only to lay them waste. He has asserted the natural Equality of Mankind, and endeavoured to suppress that Pride which inclines Men to imagine that Right is the Consequence of Power*.

> * Learn, future Natives of this promis'd Land,
> What your Fore-fathers ow'd my saving Hand!
> Learn, when *Despair* such sudden Bliss shall see,
> Such Bliss must shine from OGLETHORPE or ᵃ ME!
> Do you the neighb'ring, blameless *Indian* aid,
> Culture what he neglects, not his invade;
> Dare not, oh! dare not, with ambitious View,
> Force or demand Subjection, never due.
> Let by *my* specious Name no *Tyrants* rise,
> And cry, while they enslave, they civilize! [...]
> Why must I *Afric*'s sable Children see
> Vended for Slaves, though form'd by Nature free,
> The nameless Tortures cruel Minds invent,
> Those to subject, whom Nature equal meant?
> If these you dare, albeit unjust Success
> Empow'rs you now unpunish'd to oppress,
> Revolving Empire you and yours may doom;
> *Rome* all subdued, yet *Vandals* vanquish'd *Rome*:
> Yes, Empire may revolve, give them the Day,
> And Yoke may Yoke, and Blood may Blood repay.

ᵃ *Publick Spirit.*

His Description of the various Miseries which force Men to seek for Refuge in distant Countries affords another Instance of his Proficiency in the important and extensive Study of human Life, and the Tenderness with which he recounts them, another Proof of his Humanity and Benevolence.

It is observable, that the Close of this Poem discovers a Change which Experience had made in Mr. *Savage's* Opinions. In a Poem written by him in his Youth, and published in his Miscellanies, he declares his Contempt of the contracted Views and narrow Prospects of the middle State of Life, and declares his Resolution either to tower like the Cedar, or be trampled like the Shrub[66]; but in this Poem, though addressed to a Prince, he mentions this State of Life as comprising those who ought most to attract Reward, those who merit most the Confidence of Power, and the Familiarity of Greatness, and accidentally mentioning this Passage to one of his Friends, declared that in his Opinion all the Virtue of Mankind was comprehended in that State.

In describing Villas and Gardens he did not omit to condemn that absurd Custom which prevails among the *English* of permitting Servants to receive Money from Strangers for the Entertainment that they receive, and therefore inserted in his Poem these Lines:

> But what the flow'ring Pride of Gardens rare,
> However royal, or however fair:
> If Gates which to access should still give Way,
> Ope but, like *Peter's* Paradise, for Pay;
> If perquisited Varlets frequent stand,
> And each new Walk must a new Tax demand?
> What foreign Eye but with Contempt surveys?
> What Muse shall from Oblivion snatch their Praise?

[66] The poem written in his youth is 'To a Young Gentleman, a Painter' (*Plain Dealer*, no. 15, 1724). Savage revised it in 1737, reversing his opinions on the 'middle state of life' (i.e. the middle classes).

But before the Publication of his Performance he recollected, that the Queen allowed her Garden and Cave at *Richmond* to be shewn for Money, and that she so openly countenanced the Practice, that she had bestowed the Privilege of shewing them as a Place of Profit on a Man whose Merit she valued herself upon rewarding, though she gave him only the Liberty of disgracing his Country.

He therefore thought, with more Prudence than was often exerted by him, that the Publication of these Lines might be officiously represented as an Insult upon the Queen to whom he owed his Life and his Subsistence, and that the Propriety of his Observation would be no Security against the Censures which the Unseasonableness of it might draw upon him; he therefore suppressed the Passage in the first Edition, but after the Queen's Death thought the same Caution no longer necessary, and restored it to the proper Place.

The Poem was therefore published without any political Faults, and inscribed to the Prince, but Mr. *Savage* having no Friend upon whom he could prevail to present it to him, had no other Method of attracting his Observation than the Publication of frequent Advertisements, and therefore received no Reward from his Patron, however generous on other Occasions.

This Disappointment he never mentioned without Indignation, being by some Means or other confident that the Prince was not ignorant of his Address to him, and insinuated, that if any Advances in Popularity could have been made by distinguishing him, he had not written without Notice, or without Reward.

He was once inclined to have presented his Poem in Person, and sent to the Printer for a Copy with that Design; but either his Opinion changed, or his Resolution deserted him, and he continued to resent Neglect without attempting to force himself into Regard.

Nor was the Public much more favourable than his Patron, for only seventy-two were sold, though the Performance was much commended by some whose Judgment in that Kind of Writing is generally allowed. But *Savage* easily reconciled himself to Mankind without imputing any Defect to his Work, by observing that his Poem was unluckily published two Days after the Prorogation of the Parliament, and by Consequence at a Time when all those who could be expected to regard it were in the Hurry of preparing for their Departure, or engaged in taking Leave of others upon their Dismission from public Affairs.

It must be however allowed, in Justification of the Public, that this Performance is not the most excellent of Mr. *Savage*'s Works, and that though it cannot be denied to contain many striking Sentiments, majestic Lines, and just Observations, it is in general not sufficiently polished in the Language, or enlivened in the Imagery, or digested in the Plan.

Thus his Poem contributed nothing to the Alleviation of his Poverty, which was such as very few could have supported with equal Patience, but to which it must likewise be confessed, that few would have been exposed who received punctually fifty Pounds a Year; a Salary which though by no Means equal to the Demands of Vanity and Luxury, is yet found sufficient to support Families above Want, and was undoubtedly more than the Necessities of Life require.[67]

But no sooner had he received his Pension, than he withdrew to his darling Privacy, from which he return'd in a short Time to his former Distress, and for some Part of the Year, generally lived by Chance, eating only when he was invited to the Tables of his Acquaintances, from which the Meanness of his Dress often excluded him, when the Polite-

[67] Since Johnson had made the acquaintance of Savage some time between the publication of the first edition of *Of Public Spirit* (1737) and that of the second (1739), he was from here on able to write largely from personal knowledge.

ness and Variety of his Conversation would have been thought a sufficient Recompence for his Entertainment.

He lodged as much by Accident as he dined and passed the Night, sometimes in mean Houses, which are set open at Night to any casual Wanderers, sometimes in Cellars among the Riot and Filth of the meanest and most profligate of the Rabble; and sometimes, when he had no Money to support even the Expences of these Receptacles, walked about the Streets till he was weary, and lay down in the Summer upon a Bulk, or in the Winter with his Associates in Poverty, among the Ashes of a Glass-house.

In this Manner were passed those Days and those Nights, which Nature had enabled him to have employed in elevated Speculations, useful Studies, or pleasing Conversation. On a Bulk, in a Cellar, or in a Glass-house among Thieves and Beggars,[68] was to be found the Author of the *Wanderer*, the Man of exalted Sentiments, extensive Views and curious Observations, the Man whose Remarks on Life might have assisted the Statesman, whose Ideas of Virtue might have enlightned the Moralist, whose Eloquence might have influenced Senates, and whose Delicacy might have polished Courts.

It cannot be imagined but that such Necessities might sometimes force him upon disreputable Practices, and it is probable that these Lines in the *Wanderer* were occasioned by his Reflections on his own Conduct.

> Though Mis'ry leads to Fortitude and Truth,
> Unequal to the Load this languid Youth, [...]
> (O! let none Censure if untried by Grief,
> Or amidst Woes untempted by Relief,)
> He stoop'd, reluctant, to mean Acts of Shame,
> Which then, ev'n then, he scorn'd, and blush'd to name.[69]

---

[68] 'It is more properly written *begger*; but the common orthography is retained, because the derivations all preserve the *a*' (*Dictionary*). In 44 Johnson had spelled it with an *e*, but it was changed to *a* in 48.

[69] *Wanderer*, iii. 265–72.

Whoever was acquainted with him, was certain to be solicited for small Sums, which the Frequency of the Request made in Time considerable, and he was therefore quickly shunned by those who were become familiar enough to be trusted with his Necessities; but his rambling Manner of Life, and constant Appearance at Houses of public Resort, always procured him a new Succession of Friends, whose Kindness had not been exhausted by repeated Requests, so that he was seldom absolutely without Resources, but had in his utmost Exigences this Comfort, that he always imagined himself sure of speedy Relief.

It was observed that he always asked Favours of this Kind without the least Submission or apparent Consciousness of Dependence, and that he did not seem to look upon a Compliance with his Request as an Obligation that deserved any extraordinary Acknowledgments, but a Refusal was resented by him as an Affront, or complained of as an Injury; nor did he readily reconcile himself to those who either denied to lend, or gave him afterwards any Intimation, that they expected to be repaid.

He was sometimes so far compassionated by those who knew both his Merit and his Distresses, that they received him into their Families, but they soon discovered him to be a very incommodious Inmate; for being always accustomed to an irregular Manner of Life, he could not confine himself to any stated Hours, or pay any Regard to the Rules of a Family, but would prolong his Conversation till Midnight, without considering that Business might require his Friend's Application in the Morning; nor when he had persuaded himself to retire to Bed, was he, without Difficulty, called up to Dinner; it was therefore impossible to pay him any Distinction without the entire Subversion of all Oeconomy, a Kind of Establishment which, wherever he went, he always appeared ambitious to overthrow.

It must therefore be acknowledged, in Justification of

Mankind, that it was not always by the Negligence or Coldness of his Friends that *Savage* was distressed, but because it was in reality very difficult to preserve him long in a State of Ease. To supply him with Money was a hopeless Attempt, for no sooner did he see himself Master of a Sum sufficient to set him free from Care for a Day, than he became profuse and luxurious. When once he had entred a Tavern, or engaged in a Scheme of Pleasure, he never retired till Want of Money obliged him to some new Expedient. If he was entertained in a Family, nothing was any longer to be regarded there but Amusements and Jollity; wherever *Savage* entered he immediately expected that Order and Business should fly before him, that all should thenceforward be left to Hazard, and that no dull Principle of domestic Management should be opposed to his Inclination, or intrude upon his Gaiety.

His Distresses, however afflictive, never dejected him; in his lowest State he wanted not Spirit to assert the natural Dignity of Wit, and was always ready to repress that Insolence which Superiority of Fortune incited, and to trample the Reputation which rose upon any other Basis than that of Merit: He never admitted any gross Familiarities, or submitted to be treated otherwise than as an equal. Once when he was without Lodging, Meat, or Cloaths, one of his Friends, a Man not indeed remarkable for Moderation in his Prosperity, left a Message, that he desired to see him about nine in the Morning. *Savage* knew that his Intention was to assist him, but was very much disgusted, that he should presume to prescribe the Hour of his Attendance, and, I believe, refused to visit him, and rejected his Kindness.

The same invincible Temper, whether Firmness or Obstinacy, appeared in his Conduct to the Lord *Tyrconnel*, from whom he very frequently demanded that the Allowance which was once paid him should be restored, but with whom he never appeared to entertain for a Moment the

Thought of soliciting a Reconciliation, and whom he treated at once with all the Haughtiness of Superiority, and all the Bitterness of Resentment. He wrote to him not in a Stile of Supplication or Respect, but of Reproach, Menace, and Contempt, and appeared determined, if he ever regained his Allowance, to hold it only by the Right of Conquest.[70]

As many more can discover, that a Man is richer than that he is wiser than themselves, Superiority of Understanding is not so readily acknowledged as that of Condition; nor is that Haughtiness, which the Consciousness of great Abilities incites, borne with the same Submission as the Tyranny of Wealth; and therefore *Savage*, by asserting his Claim to Deference and Regard, and by treating those with Contempt whom better Fortune animated to rebel against him, did not fail to raise a great Number of Enemies in the different Classes of Mankind. Those who thought themselves raised above him by the Advantages of Riches, hated him because they found no Protection from the Petulance of his Wit. Those who were esteemed for their Writings feared him as a Critic, and maligned him as a Rival, and almost all the smaller Wits were his professed Enemies.

Among these Mr. *Millar* so far indulged his Resentment as to introduce him in a Farce, and direct him to be personated on the Stage in a Dress like that which he then wore; a mean Insult which only insinuated, that *Savage* had but one Coat, and which was therefore despised by him rather than resented; for though he wrote a Lampoon against *Millar*, he never printed it: and as no other Person ought to prosecute that Revenge from which the Person who was

[70] Cf. letter from Pope to Savage, 15 Sept. 1742: 'What mortal would take . . . your business with Lord T. out of your hands, if you could come, and attend it yourself? . . . And what was done more in relation to the Lord, but trying a method we thought more likely to serve you, than threats and injurious language? . . . I was shocked at your strong declarations of *vengeance* and *violent measures* against him. . . .' (*Correspondence of Alexander Pope*, ed. George Sherburn (Oxford, 1956), iv, 417–18).

injured desisted, I shall not preserve what Mr. *Savage* suppressed; of which the Publication would indeed have been
a Punishment too severe for so impotent an Assault.[71]

   The great Hardships of Poverty were to *Savage* not the
Want of Lodging or of Food, but the Neglect and Contempt
which it drew upon him. He complained that as his Affairs
grew desperate he found his Reputation for Capacity visibly
decline, that his Opinion in Questions of Criticism was no
longer regarded, when his Coat was out of Fashion; and
that those who in the Interval of his Prosperity were always
encouraging him to great Undertakings by Encomiums on
his Genius and Assurances of Success, now received any
Mention of his Designs with Coldness, thought that the
Subjects on which he proposed to write were very difficult;
and were ready to inform him, that the Event of a Poem
was uncertain, that an Author ought to employ much Time
in the Consideration of his Plan, and not presume to sit

---

[71] James Miller (1706–44) wrote a number of farcical comedies, in two
of which a poet made an appearance: the *Mother-in-Law* (Feb. 1734) and
the *Coffee-House* (Jan. 1738). In the former a poet appeared briefly and
with no motivation in the plot, evidently in order to take off somebody
whom the audience would recognize. Pointed reference was made to his
dress:

   POET. For my part, Sir, I should have been glad if some person of taste
   and understanding had told you what I am.

   BEAUMONT. O Sir! that's visible in your dress and behaviour; you are
   a poet I presume, Sir.

Moreover, he was arrogant and contemptuous of other poets; he tried
to force a patron to accept the dedication of his latest tragedy; he left
a number of tickets for the performance; and he was got rid of at last
only at the cost of two guineas—in short, a by no means unrecognizable
take-off on Savage. But when the *Mother-in-Law* was performed Savage
ought not to have been suffering from want, though even two substantial
pensions probably did not keep him in funds. This difficulty does not
arise, however, over the *Coffee-House*, a brief ballad-opera, in which
one of the principal characters, Bays, a poet, was compelled to write his
verses in a coffee-house for want of anywhere else to go, was in debt,
threatened to write satires about people who offended him, and insisted
on reading a tragedy of his own composition to Cibber, who happened
to have dropped in. But no reference was made in the text to the poet's
clothes.

down to write in Confidence of a few cursory Ideas, and a superficial Knowledge; Difficulties were started on all Sides, and he was no longer qualified for any Performance but the *Volunteer Laureat.*

Yet even this Kind of Contempt never depressed him; for he always preserved a steady Confidence in his own Capacity, and believed nothing above his Reach which he should at any Time earnestly endeavour to attain. He formed Schemes of the same Kind with regard to Knowledge and to Fortune, and flattered himself with Advances to be made in Science, as with Riches to be enjoyed in some distant Period of his Life. For the Acquisition of Knowledge he was indeed far better qualified than for that of Riches; for he was naturally inquisitive and desirous of the Conversation of those from whom any Information was to be obtained, but by no Means solicitous to improve those Opportunities that were sometimes offered of raising his Fortune; and was remarkably retentive of his Ideas, which, when once he was in Possession of them, rarely forsook him; a Quality which could never be communicated to his Money.

While he was thus wearing out his Life in Expectation that the Queen would some time recollect her Promise, he had Recourse to the usual Practice of Writers, and published Proposals for printing his Works by Subscription, to which he was encouraged by the Success of many who had not a better Right to the Favour of the Public; but whatever was the Reason, he did not find the World equally inclined to favour him, and he observed with some Discontent, that though he offered his Works at half a Guinea, he was able to procure but a small Number in Comparison with those who subscribed twice as much to *Duck.*[72]

[72] The proposals published in *GM*. 37. 128 promise an edition in large octavo on fine paper, which will contain 'several pieces in prose and verse, humorous, serious, moral and divine, never before printed'. Cf. pp. 80, 111. Stephen Duck (1705–56), the Thresher Poet, dedicated his *Poems on*

Nor was it without Indignation that he saw his Proposals neglected by the Queen, who patronised Mr. *Duck*'s with uncommon Ardour, and incited a Competition among those who attended the Court, who should most promote his Interest, and who should first offer a Subscription. This was a Distinction to which Mr. *Savage* made no Scruple of asserting that his Birth, his Misfortunes, and his Genius gave him a fairer Title, than could be pleaded by him on whom it was conferred.

Savage's Applications were however not universally unsuccessful; for some of the Nobility countenanced his Design, encouraged his Proposals, and subscribed with great Liberality. He related of the Duke of *Chandos* particularly, that, upon receiving his Proposals, he sent him ten Guineas.

But the Money which his Subscriptions afforded him was not less volatile than that which he received from his other Schemes; whenever a Subscription was paid him he went to a Tavern, and as Money so collected is necessarily received in small Sums, he never was able to send his Poems to the Press, but for many Years continued his Solicitation, and squandered whatever he obtained.

This Project of printing his Works was frequently revived, and as his Proposals grew obsolete, new ones were printed with fresher Dates. To form Schemes for the Publication was one of his favourite Amusements, nor was he ever more at Ease than when with any Friend who readily fell in with his Schemes, he was adjusting the Print, forming the Advertisements, and regulating the Dispersion of his new Edition, which he really intended some time to publish, and which, as long Experience had shewn him the Impossibility of printing the Volume together, he at last determined to divide into weekly or monthly Numbers, that the Profits of the first might supply the Expences of the next.

Several Occasions in 1736 to the Queen and printed a list of over 500 subscribers, including the names of many lords and ladies as well as those of Pope, Swift, and Joseph Spence.

Thus he spent his Time in mean Expedients and tormenting Suspense, living for the greatest Part in Fear of Prosecutions from his Creditors, and consequently skulking in obscure Parts of the Town, of which he was no Stranger to the remotest Corners. But wherever he came his Address secured him Friends, whom his Necessities soon alienated, so that he had perhaps a more numerous Acquaintance than any Man ever before attained, there being scarcely any Person eminent on any Account to whom he was not known, or whose Character he was not in some Degree able to delineate.

To the Acquisition of this extensive Acquaintance every Circumstance of his Life contributed. He excelled in the Arts of Conversation, and therefore willingly practised them: He had seldom any Home, or even a Lodging in which he could be private, and therefore was driven into public Houses for the common Conveniences of Life, and Supports of Nature.[73] He was always ready to comply with every Invitation, having no Employment to withhold him, and often no Money to provide for himself; and by dining with one Company, he never failed of obtaining an Introduction into another.

Thus dissipated[74] was his Life, and thus casual his Subsistence; yet did not the Distraction of his Views hinder him from Reflection, nor the Uncertainty of his Condition depress his Gaiety. When he had wandered about without any fortunate Adventure, by which he was led into a Tavern, he sometimes retired into the Fields, and was able to employ his Mind in Study to amuse it with pleasing Imaginations; and seldom appeared to be melancholy, but when some sudden Misfortune had just fallen upon him, and even

[73] In the copy in the Euing Collection in the Library of the University of Glasgow, Johnson has written in the bottom margin: 'The old woman'. It is impossible to say to what he referred. Perhaps he was trying to identify in his memory the source of some information given on this page.

[74] Cf. p. 137 and n.

then in a few Moments he would disentangle himself from his Perplexity, adopt the Subject of Conversation, and apply his Mind wholly to the Objects that others presented to it.

This Life, unhappy as it may be already imagined, was yet imbitter'd in 1738, with new Calamities. The Death of the Queen deprived him of all the Prospects of Preferment with which he had so long entertained his Imagination;[75] and as Sir *Robert Walpole* had before given him Reason to believe that he never intended the Performance of his Promise, he was now abandoned again to Fortune.

He was, however at that time, supported by a Friend; and as it was not his Custom to look out for distant Calamities, or to feel any other Pain than that which forced itself upon his Senses, he was not much afflicted at his Loss, and perhaps comforted himself that his Pension would be now continued without the annual Tribute of a Panegyric.

Another Expectation contributed likewise to support him; he had taken a Resolution to write a second Tragedy upon the Story of Sir *Thomas Overbury*, in which he preserved a few Lines of his former Play; but made a total Alteration of the Plan, added new Incidents, and introduced new Characters; so that it was a new Tragedy, not a Revival of the former.[76]

---

[75] Queen Caroline died on 20 Nov. 1737. Immediately afterwards the King gave express orders that all her charitable benefactions were to be continued, and it was not until Sept. 1738 that Savage learned that his name had been cut off the list (Sloane MS. 4318, f. 46). Johnson's narrative is foreshortened, and so creates the false impression that the Queen died in 1738.

[76] Savage took the manuscript of this play with him to Wales and Bristol, where it was recovered in 1749 thanks to Tho. Cadell, a Bristol bookseller, who declared that it was perfect when he sent it to Edward Cave in London (*Poetical Works of Richard Savage*, ed. Clarence Tracy (Cambridge, 1962), p. 9 n). In 1777 the play was produced at the Theatre Royal, Covent Garden; not, however, in the condition in which the author had left it, but in a version by William Woodfall, who remarked in his introductory note that the play had been incomplete when he received it, lacking the final act, and that he had had to do a good deal of polishing and transposing to make it actable. The manuscript, the only Savage

Many of his Friends blamed him for not making Choice of another Subject; but in Vindication of himself, he asserted, that it was not easy to find a better; and that he thought it his Interest to extinguish the Memory of the first Tragedy, which he could only do by writing one less defective upon the same Story; by which he should entirely defeat the Artifice of the Booksellers, who after the Death of any Author of Reputation, are always industrious to swell his Works, by uniting his worst Productions with his best.

In the Execution of this Scheme however, he proceeded but slowly, and probably only employed himself upon it when he could find no other Amusement; but he pleased himself with counting the Profits, and perhaps imagined, that the theatrical Reputation which he was about to acquire, would be equivalent to all that he had lost by the Death of his Patroness.

He did not in Confidence of his approaching Riches neglect the Measures proper to secure the Continuance of his Pension, though some of his Favourers thought him culpable for omitting to write on her Death; but on her Birth Day next Year, he gave a Proof of the Solidity of his Judgment, and the Power of his Genius.

He knew that the Track of Elegy had been so long beaten, that it was impossible to travel in it without treading in the Footsteps of those who had gone before him; and that therefore it was necessary that he might distinguish himself from the Herd of Encomiasts, to find out some new Walk of funeral Panegyric.

This difficult Task he performed in such a Manner, that his Poem may be justly ranked among the best Pieces that

literary manuscript still surviving, is now in the Hyde Collection in New Jersey. It appears to be made up of a copy of the printed play with extensive alterations in holograph on inserted leaves—written in more than one hand.

the Death of Princes has produced.[77] By transferring the Mention of her Death to her Birth Day, he has formed a happy Combination of Topics which any other Man would have thought it very difficult to connect in one View; but which he has united in such a Manner, that the Relation between them appears natural; and it may be justly said that what no other Man would have thought on, it now appears scarcely possible for any Man to miss*.

* To exhibit a Specimen of the Beauties of this Poem, the following Passages are selected.

> Oft has the Muse, on this distinguish'd Day,
> Tun'd to glad Harmony the vernal Lay;
> But, O lamented Change! The Lay must flow
> From grateful Rapture now, to grateful Woe.
> She, to this Day, who joyous Lustre gave,
> Descends for ever to the silent Grave.
> She born at once to charm us and to mend,
> Of human Race the Pattern and the Friend.
> ——And, thou, bright Princess! seated now on high,
> Next one, the fairest Daughter of the Sky,
> Whose warm-felt Love is to all Beings known,
> Thy Sister *Charity*! next her thy Throne;
> See at thy Tomb the Virtues weeping lie!
> There in dumb Sorrow seem the Arts to die.
> So were the Sun o'er other Orbs to blaze,
> And from our World, like thee, withdraw his Rays,
> No more to visit where he warm'd before,
> All Life must cease, and Nature be no more.
> Yet shall the MUSE a heav'nly Height essay,
> Beyond the Weakness mix'd with mortal Clay;
> Beyond the Loss, which, tho' she bleeds to see,
> Tho' ne'er to be redeem'd the Loss of thee;
> Beyond ev'n this, she hails with joyous Lay,
> Thy better Birth, thy first true natal Day;
> A Day, that sees Thee born, beyond the Tomb,
> To endless Health, to Youth's eternal Bloom.
> Born to the mighty Dead, the Souls sublime
> Of ev'ry famous Age, and ev'ry Clime,
> To Goodness fixed by Truth's unvarying Laws;
> To Bliss that knows no Period, knows no Pause——
> Save when thine Eye, from yonder pure Serene,
> Sheds a soft Ray on this our gloomy Scene.

[77] *Volunteer Laureat,* no. 7, 1 Mar. 1738. Published before Savage learned that his pension was not to be continued.

The Beauty of this peculiar Combination of Images is so masterly, that it is sufficient to set this Poem above Censure; and therefore it is not necessary to mention many other delicate Touches which may be found in it, and which would deservedly be admired in any other Performance.

To these Proofs of his Genius may be added, from the same Poem, an Instance of his Prudence, an Excellence for which he was not so often distinguished; he does not forget * to remind the King in the most delicate and artful Manner of continuing his Pension.

With regard to the Success of this Address he was for some Time in Suspense; but was in no great Degree sollicitous about it; and continued his Labour upon his new Tragedy with great Tranquillity, till the Friend, who had for a considerable time supported him, removing his Family to another Place, took Occasion to dismiss him. It then became necessary to enquire more diligently what was determined in his Affair, having Reason to suspect that no great Favour was intended him, because he had not received his Pension at the usual Time.

It is said, that he did not take those Methods of retrieving his Interest which were most likely to succeed; and some of those who were employed in the Exchequer, cautioned him against too much Violence in his Proceedings; but Mr. *Savage* who seldom regulated his Conduct by the Advice of others, gave way to his Passion, and demanded of Sir *Robert Walpole*, at his Levee, the Reason of the Distinction that was made between him and the other Pensioners of the Queen, with a Degree of Roughness which

* ——Deign one Look more! Ah! See thy Consort dear!
Wishing all Hearts, except his own, to cheer.
Lo! still he bids thy wonted Bounties flow
To weeping Families of Worth and Woe.
He stops all Tears, however fast they rise,
Save those, that still must fall from grateful Eyes:
And spite of Griefs, that so usurp his Mind,
Still watches o'er the Welfare of Mankind.

perhaps determined him to withdraw what had been only delayed.

Whatever was the Crime of which he was accused or suspected, and whatever Influence was imployed against him, he received soon after an Account that took from him all Hopes of regaining his Pension; and he had now no Prospect of Subsistence but from his Play, and he knew no Way of Living for the Time required to finish it.

So peculiar were the Misfortunes of this Man, deprived of an Estate and Title by a particular Law, exposed and abandoned by a Mother, defrauded by a Mother of a Fortune which his Father had allotted him, he enter'd the World without a Friend; and though his Abilities forced themselves into Esteem and Reputation, he was never able to obtain any real Advantage, and whatever Prospects arose, were always intercepted as he began to approach them. The King's Intentions in his Favour were frustrated; his Dedication to the Prince, whose Generosity on every other Occasion was eminent, procured him no Reward; Sir *Robert Walpole* who valued himself upon keeping his Promise to others, broke it to him without Regret; and the Bounty of the Queen was, after her Death, withdrawn from him, and from him only.

Such were his Misfortunes, which yet he bore not only with Decency, but with Cheerfulness, nor was his Gaiety clouded even by his last Disappointment, though he was in a short Time reduced to the lowest Degree of Distress, and often wanted both Lodging and Food. At this Time he gave another Instance of the insurmountable Obstinacy of his Spirit; his Cloaths were worn out, and he received Notice that at a Coffee-House some Cloaths and Linen were left for him; the Person who sent them, did not, I believe, inform him to whom he was to be obliged, that he might spare the Perplexity of acknowledging the Benefit; but though the Offer was so far generous, it was made with some Neglect of

Ceremonies, which Mr. *Savage* so much resented, that he refused the Present, and declined to enter the House, till the Cloaths that had been designed for him were taken away.

His Distress was now publickly known, and his Friends, therefore, thought it proper to concert some Measures for his Relief; and one of them[78] wrote a Letter to him, in which he expressed his Concern *for the miserable withdrawing of his Pension*; and gave him Hopes that in a short Time, he should find himself supplied with a Competence, *without any Dependence on those little Creatures which we are pleased to call the Great.*

The Scheme proposed for this happy and independent Subsistence, was, that he should retire into *Wales*, and receive an Allowance of fifty Pounds a Year, to be raised by a Subscription,[79] on which he was to live privately in a cheap Place, without aspiring any more to Affluence, or having any farther Care of Reputation.

This Offer Mr. *Savage* gladly accepted, tho' with Intentions very different from those of his Friends; for they proposed, that he should continue an Exile from *London* for ever, and spend all the remaining Part of his Life at *Swansea*; but he designed only to take the Opportunity, which their Scheme offered him, of retreating for a short Time, that he might prepare his Play for the Stage, and his other Works for the Press, and then to return to *London* to exhibit his Tragedy, and live upon the Profits of his own Labour.

With regard to his Works, he proposed very great Im-

[78] In the margin opposite these words in the Euing copy Johnson wrote: 'Pope'. The reason for his withholding Pope's name here and elsewhere has been discussed in the Textual Introduction.

[79] The other benefactors were Pope's friends: Ralph Allen, Erasmus Lewis, Solomon Mendes, and possibly Dodsley (cf. p. 115 n.) as well as a group of small contributors rounded up by David Mallet. (Cf. *AB*, pp. 136–9; and see *Correspondence of Pope*, iv. 209–10, 417–18; *Philological Quarterly*, xxxvi (1957), 508–11.) At first the full amount was probably raised, but, after some of the other subscribers withdrew, Pope most likely made up the deficiencies so far as he could, no doubt subscribing on an average the £20 mentioned by both Ayre and Johnson. Cf. p. 114.

provements, which would have required much Time, or great Application; and when he had finish'd them, he designed to do Justice to his Subscribers, by publishing them according to his Proposals.

As he was ready to entertain himself with future Pleasures, he had planned out a Scheme of Life for the Country, of which he had no Knowledge but from Pastorals and Songs. He imagined that he should be transported to Scenes of flow'ry Felicity, like those which one Poet has reflected to another, and had projected a perpetual Round of innocent Pleasures, of which he suspected no Interruption from Pride, or Ignorance, or Brutality.

With these Expectations he was so enchanted, that when he was once gently reproach'd by a Friend for submitting to live upon a Subscription, and advised rather by a resolute Exertion of his Abilities to support himself, he could not bear to debar himself from the Happiness which was to be found in the Calm of a Cottage, or lose the Opportunity of listening without Intermission, to the Melody of the Nightingale, which he believ'd was to be heard from every Bramble, and which he did not fail to mention as a very important Part of the Happiness of a Country Life.

While this Scheme was ripening, his Friends directed him to take a Lodging in the Liberties of the Fleet,[80] that he might be secure from his Creditors, and sent him every Monday a Guinea, which he commonly spent before the next Morning, and trusted, after his usual Manner, the remaining Part of the Week to the Bounty of Fortune.

He now began very sensibly to feel the Miseries of Dependence: Those by whom he was to be supported, began to prescribe to him with an Air of Authority, which he knew not how decently to resent, nor patiently to bear; and he soon discovered from the Conduct of most of his Subscribers, that he was yet in the Hands of *Little Creatures*.

[80] A section of what is now central London, in which debtors could not be arrested.

Of the Insolence that he was obliged to suffer, he gave many Instances, of which none appeared to raise his Indignation to a greater Height, than the Method which was taken of furnishing him with Cloaths. Instead of consulting him and allowing him to send to a Taylor his Orders for what they thought proper to allow him, they proposed to send for a Taylor to take his Measure, and then to consult how they should equip him.

This Treatment was not very delicate, nor was it such as *Savage*'s Humanity would have suggested to him on a like Occasion; but it had scarcely deserved mention, had it not, by affecting him in an uncommon Degree, shewn the Peculiarity of his Character. Upon hearing the Design that was formed, he came to the Lodging of a Friend with the most violent Agonies of Rage; and being asked what it could be that gave him such Disturbance, he replied with the utmost Vehemence of Indignation, 'That they had sent for a Taylor to measure him.'

How the Affair ended, was never enquired, for fear of renewing his Uneasiness. It is probable that, upon Recollection, he submitted with a good Grace to what he could not avoid, and that he discovered no Resentment where he had no Power.

He was, however, not humbled to implicit and universal Compliance; for when the Gentleman, who had first informed him of the Design to support him by a Subscription, attempted to procure a Reconciliation with the Lord *Tyrconnel*, he could by no Means be prevailed upon to comply with the Measures that were proposed.

A Letter was written for him*[81] to Sir *William Lemon*, to

* By Mr. *Pope*.

[81] In the margin opposite these words in the Euing copy Johnson wrote: 'by Pope'. The footnote was not added until 1775. Sir William Leman had recently married Mrs. Brett's daughter by Colonel Brett (*GM.* 37. 637). When Pope wrote 'so small a Relation' he meant 'so brief an account'.

prevail upon him to interpose his good Offices with Lord *Tyrconnel*, in which he solicited Sir *William*'s Assistance, *for a Man who really needed it as much as any Man could well do*; and informed him, that he was retiring *for ever to a Place where he should no more trouble his Relations, Friends, or Enemies*; he confessed, that his *Passion* had *betrayed* him to some Conduct, with Regard to Lord *Tyrconnel, for which he could not but heartily ask his Pardon*; and as he imagined Lord *Tyrconnel*'s Passion might be yet so high, that he would not *receive a Letter from him*, begg'd that Sir *William* would endeavour to soften him; and expressed his Hopes, that he would comply with his Request, and that *so small a Relation would not harden his Heart against him*.

That any Man should presume to dictate a Letter to him, was not very agreeable to Mr. *Savage*; and therefore he was, before he had opened it, not much inclined to approve it. But when he read it, he found it contained Sentiments entirely opposite to his own, and, as he asserted, to the Truth, and therefore instead of copying it, wrote his Friend a Letter full of masculine Resentment and warm Expostulations. He very justly observed, that the Style was too supplicatory, and the Representation too abject, and that he ought at least to have made him complain with *the Dignity of a Gentleman in Distress*. He declared that he would not write the Paragraph in which he was to ask Lord *Tyrconnel*'s Pardon; for *he despised his Pardon, and therefore could not heartily, and would not hypocritically ask it*. He remarked, that his Friend made a very unreasonable Distinction between himself and him; for, says he, when you mention Men of high Rank *in your own Character*, they are *those little Creatures whom we are pleased to call the Great*; but when you address them *in mine*, no Servility is sufficiently humble. He then with great Propriety explained the ill Consequences that might be expected from such a Letter, which his Relations would print in their own Defence, and which would for ever be produced as a full Answer to all that he should allege against them; for he always intended to publish a minute Account of the Treatment which he had received. It is to be remembered to the Honour of the Gentleman by whom this Letter was drawn up, that he yielded to Mr. *Savage*'s Reasons, and agreed that it ought to be suppressed.

After many Alterations and Delays, a Subscription was at length raised which did not amount to fifty Pounds a Year, though twenty were paid by one Gentleman[82]; such was the Generosity of Mankind, that what had been done by a Player without Solicitation, could not now be effected by Application and Interest; and *Savage* had a great Number to court and to obey for a Pension less than that which Mrs. *Oldfield* paid him without exacting any Servilities.

Mr. *Savage* however was satisfied, and willing to retire, and was convinced that the Allowance, though scanty, would be more than sufficient for him, being now determined to commence a rigid Oeconomist, and to live according to the exactest Rules of Frugality; for nothing was in his Opinion more contemptible than a Man, who, when he knew his Income, exceeded it, and yet he confessed that Instances of such Folly, were too common, and lamented, that some Men were not to be trusted with their own Money.

Full of these salutary Resolutions, he left *London*, in *July* 1739, having taken Leave with great Tenderness of his Friends, and parted from the Author of this Narrative with Tears in his Eyes.[83] He was furnished with fifteen Guineas,

---

[82] Most likely Pope, though his initial subscription was probably no more than £10. He frequently made additional contributions. Cf. p. 115; *AB*, pp. 137–8.

[83] In the margin opposite these words in the Euing copy Johnson wrote: 'I had then a slight fever'. His words in the text here are his only explicit reference to himself.

and informed, that they would be sufficient, not only for the Expence of his Journey, but for his Support in *Wales* for some Time; and that there remained but little more of the first Collection. He promised a strict Adherence to his Maxims of Parsimony, and went away in the Stage Coach; nor did his Friends expect to hear from him, till he informed them of his Arrival at *Swansea*.

But when they least expected, arrived a Letter dated the fourteenth Day after his Departure, in which he sent them Word, that he was yet upon the Road,[84] and without Money; and that he therefore could not proceed without a Remittance. They then sent him all the Money that was in their Hands, with which he was enabled to reach *Bristol*, from whence he was to go to *Swansea* by Water.

At *Bristol* he found an Embargo laid upon the Shipping, so that he could not immediately obtain a Passage[85]; and being therefore obliged to stay there some Time, he, with his usual Felicity, ingratiated himself with many of the principal Inhabitants, was invited to their Houses, distinguished at their publick Feasts, and treated with a Regard that gratify'd his Vanity, and therefore easily engaged his Affection.

He began very early after his Retirement to complain of the Conduct of his Friends in *London*, and irritated many of them so much by his Letters, that they withdrew, however honourably, their Contributions; and it is believed, that little more was paid him than the twenty Pounds a Year, which were allowed him by the Gentleman who proposed the Subscription.

[84] In the margin opposite these words in the Euing copy Johnson wrote: 'Dodsley'. He was perhaps noting the source of his information.

[85] John Latimer (*Annals of Bristol in the Eighteenth Century* (1893), p. 220) denied that there was an embargo, but he also made it clear that the port of Bristol was readying itself for the war with Spain that broke out in October, and so shipping might not have been available.

In December Savage promised Pope to proceed to Swansea in a few days. See Pope's letter to Mallet, 17 Dec. 1739, *Correspondence of Pope*, iv. 210.

After some Stay at *Bristol*, he retired to *Swansea*, the Place *originally* proposed for his Residence, where he lived about a Year[86] very much dissatisfied with the Diminution of his Salary; but contracted, as in other Places, Acquaintance with those who were most distinguished in that Country, among whom he has celebrated Mr *Powel* and Mrs. *Jones*,[87] by some Verses which he inserted in the *Gentleman's Magazine*.

Here he completed his Tragedy, of which two Acts were wanting when he left *London*, and was desirous of coming to Town to bring it upon the Stage. This Design was very warmly opposed, and he was advised by his chief Benefactor to put it into the Hands of Mr *Thomson* and Mr *Mallet*, that it might be fitted for the Stage, and to allow his Friends to receive the Profits, out of which an annual Pension should be paid him.

This Proposal he rejected with the utmost Contempt. He was by no Means convinced that the Judgment of those to whom he was required to submit, was superior to his own. He was now determined, as he expressed it, to be *no longer kept in Leading-strings*, and had no elevated Idea of *his Bounty*, who proposed to *pension him out of the Profits of his own Labours*.[88]

He attempted in *Wales* to promote a Subscription for his Works, and had once Hopes of Success; but in a short Time

[86] Savage announced his return from South Wales in a poem entitled 'Valentine's Day', which he published in *GM*. 42. 155, the March number. If it was written in Feb. 1741, he had stayed in Swansea only just over a year; but if it was written in 1742, his stay must have been much longer. Perhaps Savage wrote it in 1741 belatedly, and it was held over for publication in the next February number.

[87] Mr. Powell and Mrs. Jones belonged to the cream of Welsh society; Cf. *AB*, pp. 140–3. Johnson knew less about Savage's life in Wales than about any other period of his adult life. Savage cannot have written often to his London friends during this time.

[88] Writing to Mallet on 17 Dec. 1739 Pope reported Savage as having declared 'against all Measures, by which any of us pretend to put him into a *State of Infancy*, & the Care of another' (*Correspondence of Pope*, iv. 210).

afterwards, formed a Resolution of leaving that Part of the Country, to which he thought it not reasonable to be confined, for the Gratification of those, who having promised him a liberal Income, had no sooner banished him to a remote Corner, than they reduced his Allowance to a Salary scarcely equal to the Necessities of Life.

His Resentment of this Treatment, which, in his own Opinion, at least, he had not deserved, was such that he broke off all Correspondence with most of his Contributors, and appeared to consider them as Persecutors and Oppressors, and in the latter Part of his Life, declared, that their Conduct toward him, since his Departure from *London*, *had been Perfidiousness improving on Perfidiousness, and Inhumanity on Inhumanity.*

It is not to be supposed, that the Necessities of Mr *Savage* did not sometimes incite him to satirical Exaggerations of the Behaviour of those by whom he thought himself reduced to them. But it must be granted, that the Diminution of his Allowance was a great Hardship, and, that those who withdrew their Subscription from a Man, who, upon the Faith of their Promise, had gone into a Kind of Banishment, and abandoned all those by whom he had been before relieved in his Distresses, will find it no easy Task to vindicate their Conduct.

It may be alleged, and, perhaps, justly, that he was petulant and contemptuous, that he more frequently reproached his Subscribers for not giving him more, than thanked them for what he had received; but it is to be remembred, that his Conduct, and this is the worst Charge that can be drawn up against him, did them no real Injury; and that it, therefore, ought rather to have been pitied than resented, at least, the Resentment that it might provoke ought to have been generous and manly; Epithets which his Conduct will hardly deserve, that starves the Man whom he has persuaded to put himself into his Power.

It might have been reasonably demanded by *Savage*, that they should, before they had taken away what they promised, have replaced him in his former State, that they should have taken no Advantages from the Situation to which the Appearance of their Kindness had reduced him, and that he should have been re-called to *London*, before he was abandoned. He might justly represent, that he ought to have been considered as a Lion in the Toils, and demand to be released before the Dogs should be loosed upon him.

He endeavoured, indeed, to release himself, and with an Intent to return to *London*, went to *Bristol*, where a Repetition of the Kindness which he had formerly found, invited him to stay. He was not only caressed and treated, but had a Collection made for him of about thirty Pounds, with which it had been happy if he had immediately departed for *London*; but his Negligence did not suffer him to consider, that such Proofs of Kindness were not often to be expected, and that this Ardour of Benevolence was in a great Degree, the Effect of Novelty, and might, probably, be every Day less; and, therefore, he took no Care to improve the happy Time, but was encouraged by one Favour to hope for another, till at length Generosity was exhausted, and Officiousness wearied.

Another Part of his Misconduct was the Practice of prolonging his Visits, to unseasonable Hours, and disconcerting all the Families into which he was admitted. This was an Error in a Place of Commerce which all the Charms of his Conversation could not compensate; for what Trader would purchase such airy Satisfaction by the Loss of solid Gain, which must be the Consequence of Midnight Merriment, as those Hours which were gained at Night, were generally lost in the Morning?

Thus Mr *Savage*, after the Curiosity of the Inhabitants was gratified, found the Number of his Friends daily decreasing, perhaps without suspecting for what Reason their

Conduct was altered, for he still continued to harrass, with his nocturnal Intrusions, those that yet countenanced him, and admitted him to their Houses.

But he did not spend all the Time of his Residence at *Bristol*, in Visits or at Taverns; for he sometimes returned to his Studies, and began several considerable Designs. When he felt an Inclination to write, he always retired from the Knowledge of his Friends, and lay hid in an obscure Part of the Suburbs, till he found himself again desirous of Company, to which it is likely that Intervals of Absence made him more welcome.

He was always full of his Design of returning to *London* to bring his Tragedy upon the Stage; but having neglected to depart with the Money that was raised for him, he could not afterwards procure a Sum sufficient to defray the Expences of his Journey; nor, perhaps, would a fresh Supply have had any other Effect, than, by putting immediate Pleasures in his Power, to have driven the Thoughts of his Journey out of his Mind.

While he was thus spending the Day in contriving a Scheme for the Morrow, Distress stole upon him by imperceptible Degrees. His Conduct had already wearied some of those who were at first enamoured of his Conversation; but he might, perhaps, still have devolved to others, whom he might have entertained with equal Success, had not the Decay of his Cloaths made it no longer consistent with their Vanity to admit him to their Tables, or to associate with him in publick Places. He now began to find every Man from home at whose House he called; and was, therefore, no longer able to procure the Necessaries of Life, but wandered about the Town slighted and neglected, in quest of a Dinner, which he did not always obtain.

To complete his Misery, he was persued by the Officers for small Debts which he had contracted; and was, therefore, obliged to withdraw from the small Number of Friends from whom he had still Reason to hope for Favours. His Custom was to lye in Bed the greatest Part of the Day, and to go out in the Dark with the utmost Privacy, and after having paid his Visit, return again before Morning to his Lodging, which was in the Garret of an obscure Inn.

Being thus excluded on one hand, and confined on the other, he suffered the utmost Extremities of Poverty, and often fasted so long, that he was seized with Faintness, and had lost his Appetite, not being able to bear the smell of Meat, 'till the Action of his Stomach was restored by a Cordial.

In this Distress he received a Remittance of fifty[89] Pounds from *London*, with which he provided himself a decent Coat, and determined to go to *London*, but unhappily spent his Money at a favourite Tavern. Thus was he again confined to *Bristol*, where he was every Day hunted by Bailiffs. In this Exigence he once more found a Friend, who sheltered him in his House, though at the usual Inconveniences with which his Company was attended; for he could neither be persuaded to go to bed in the Night, nor to rise in the Day.

It is observable, that in these various Scenes of Misery, he was always disengaged and cheerful; he at some Times persued his Studies, and at others continued or enlarged his epistolary Correspondence, nor was he ever so far dejected as to endeavour to procure an Encrease of his Allowance, by any other Methods than Accusations and Reproaches.

He had now no longer any Hopes of Assistance from his Friends at *Bristol*, who as Merchants, and by Consequence sufficiently studious of Profit, cannot be supposed to have look'd with much Compassion upon Negligence and Ex-

[89] The first edition read 'five', but that was altered to 'fifty' in the second, which is the most authoritative text. It is, however, difficult to believe that the amount was actually so great and that Savage could have spent it all in one party at a tavern. Most of the later editions reverted to the reading 'five', but since they all derived from the first, there is no evidence that Johnson ever corrected the error. Cf. *Correspondence of Pope*, iv. 417.

travagance, or to think any Excellence equivalent to a Fault of such Consequence as Neglect of Oeconomy. It is natural to imagine, that many of those who would have relieved his real Wants, were discouraged from the Exertion of their Benevolence, by Observation of the Use which was made of their Favours, and Conviction that Relief would only be momentary, and that the same Necessity would quickly return.

At last he quitted the House of his Friend, and returned to his Lodging at the Inn, still intending to set out in a few Days for *London*, but on the tenth of *January* 1742–3, having been at Supper with two of his Friends, he was at his Return to his Lodgings arrested for a Debt of about eight Pounds, which he owed at a Coffee-House, and conducted to the House of a Sheriff's Officer.[90] The Account which he gives of this Misfortune in a Letter to one of the Gentlemen[91]

[90] Johnson gave no authority for the date of Savage's arrest, and I have found no confirmation for it. He may have merely inferred it from Savage's statement, in a letter quoted later, that he had been arrested on his birth-night. Johnson, relying on the anonymous *Life* and perhaps on information from Savage himself, had previously given that date as 10 Jan.; cf. p. 5 and n. The date may perhaps be confirmed by Savage's statement in another letter, quoted on p. 125, that he had been confined in Newgate 'ever since Monday last was Sev'n-night'. Since that letter was dated 30 Jan. (which was a Sunday in 1743), he must have been committed to Newgate on Monday 17 Jan. Now, according to Johnson again, he had previously been confined in the house of an officer for five days. If these five days are taken to be exclusive, the date of the arrest is pushed back to Tuesday 11 Jan.; and since it probably took place after midnight, it may be said to have taken place on his 'birth-night'. But admittedly these dates do not tie together very well.

He was arrested at the suit of a Mrs. Read who, according to the *Bristol Oracle and Country Intelligencer* for 19 Mar. 1743, kept a coffee-house in Princes Street. In the Rule Book of the Tolsey Court it is noted that the case of *Read* ag. *Savage* came up for hearings on 30 May, 27 June, and 6 July. There must have been earlier hearings of which no records have been found. Many of the records of Bristol courts for this period are unavailable.

[91] This must be the husband of the Mrs. S——s mentioned in the letter, who was most likely William Saunders, one of Savage's closest Bristol friends. He published complimentary verses about Savage in *GM*. 42. 597, as well as two verse imitations of Lucian. His name appears in the list of resident clergy in the *Bristol Poll Book* for 1739 and, if he is the same

with whom he had supped, is too remarkable to be omitted.

It was not a little unfortunate for me, that I spent yesterday's Evening with you; because the Hour hindered me from entering on my new Lodging; however, I have now got one; but such an one, as I believe Nobody would chuse.

I was arrested at the Suit of Mrs *Read*, just as I was going up Stairs to Bed, at Mr *Bowyer*'s; but taken in so private a Manner, that I believe Nobody at the *White Lyon* is apprised of it. Tho' I let the Officers know the Strength (or rather Weakness) of my Pocket, yet they treated me with the utmost Civility, and even when they conducted me to Confinement, 'twas in such a Manner, that I verily believe I could have escaped, which I would rather be ruined than have done; notwithstanding the whole Amount of my Finances was but three Pence halfpenny.

In the first Place I must insist, that you will industriously conceal this from Mrs S———s; because I would not have her good Nature suffer that Pain, which, I know, she would be apt to feel on this Occasion.

Next I conjure you, dear Sir, by all the Ties of Friendship, by no Means to have one uneasy Thought on my Account; but to have the same Pleasantry of Countenance and unruffled Serenity of Mind, which (God be praised!) I have in this, and have had in a much severer Calamity. Furthermore, I charge you, if you value my Friendship as truly as I do yours, *not* to utter, or even harbour the least Resentment against Mrs *Read*. I believe she has ruin'd me, but I freely forgive her; and (tho' I will never more have any Intimacy with her) would, at a due Distance, rather do her an Act of Good, than ill Will. Lastly,

man as the Wm. Saunders who matriculated at Balliol in 1732 at the age of seventeen, his father was Samuel Saunders, a clergyman living in Redcliff, Bristol (*Alumni Oxonienses*, 1715–1806). He was a minor canon of Bristol cathedral until Apr. 1743, but, according to information received from the Hon. Archivist of that cathedral, seems not to have been a success. Savage quarrelled with him, writing to a friend on 19 June 1743: 'Is the devil always to possess that worthless fellow Saunders? can he never open his mouth in conversation, but out of it must issue a lie?' And two days later: 'I cannot but smile at Saunders—he calls you "poor creature!" he stole that very expression out of my letter to him, where, with great propriety, it was applied to himself' (*GM*. 87. 1040–1).

(pardon the Expression) I *absolutely command* you not to offer me any pecuniary Assistance, nor to attempt getting me any from any one of your Friends. At another Time, or on any other Occasion, you may, dear Friend, be well assured, I would rather write to you in the submissive Stile of a Request, than that of a peremptory Command.

However, that my truly valuable Friend may not think I am too proud to ask a Favour, let me entreat you to let me have your Boy to attend me for this Day, not only for the Sake of saving me the Expence of Porters; but for the Delivery of some Letters to People, whose Names I would not have known to Strangers.

The civil Treatment I have thus far met from those, whose Prisoner I am, makes me thankful to the Almighty, that, tho' He has thought fit to visit me (on my Birth-night) with Affliction; yet (such is his great Goodness!) my Affliction is not without alleviating Circumstances. I murmur not, but am all Resignation to the *divine Will*. As to the World, I hope that I shall be endued by Heaven with that Presence of Mind, that serene Dignity in Misfortune, that constitutes the Character of a true Nobleman; a Dignity far beyond that of Coronets; a Nobility arising from the just Principles of Philosophy, refined and exalted, by those of Christianity.

He continued five Days at the Officer's, in Hopes that he should be able to procure Bail, and avoid the Necessity of going to Prison. The State in which he passed his Time, and the Treatment which he received, are very justly expressed by him in a Letter which he wrote to a Friend; 'The whole Day, *says he*, has been employed in various People's filling my Head with their foolish chimerical Systems, which has obliged me coolly (as far as Nature will admit) to digest, and accommodate myself to, every different Person's Way of thinking; hurried from one wild System to another, 'till it has quite made a Chaos of my Imagination, and nothing done—Promised—disappointed—Order'd to send every hour, from one part of the Town to the other.'———

When his Friends, who had hitherto caressed and applauded, found that to give Bail and pay the Debt was the same, they all refused to preserve him from a Prison, at the Expence of eight Pounds; and therefore after having been for some Time at the Officer's House, *at an immense Expense*, as he observes in his Letter, he was at length removed to *Newgate*.

This Expence he was enabled to support, by the Generosity of Mr *Nash* at *Bath*, who upon receiving from him an Account of his Condition, immediately sent him five Guineas, and promised to promote his Subscription at *Bath*, with all his Interest.[92]

By his Removal to *Newgate*, he obtained at least a Freedom from Suspense, and Rest from the disturbing Vicissitudes of Hope and Disappointment; he now found that his Friends were only Companions, who were willing to share his Gaiety, but not to partake of his Misfortunes; and therefore he no longer expected any Assistance from them.

It must however be observed of one Gentleman, that he offered to release him by paying the Debt, but that Mr *Savage* would not consent, I suppose, because he thought he had been before too burthensome to him.

He was offered by some of his Friends, that a Collection should be made for his Enlargement, but he *treated the Proposal*, and declared*, *that he should again treat it, with Disdain. As to writing any mendicant Letters, he had too high a Spirit, and determined only to write to some Ministers of State, to try to regain his Pension.*

He continued to complain † of those that had sent him

---

* In a Letter after his Confinement.
† Letter *Jan.* 15.

---

[92] Oliver Goldsmith did not mention this benefaction in his *Life of Nash,* and in June Savage wrote as follows to his friend Strong: 'Mr. Nash (though I wrote to him since) has never once wrote or sent to me' (*GM.* 87. 1039). Perhaps, however, Savage's 'never' is not to be taken literally, in view of his 'since'.

into the Country, and objected to them, that he had *lost the Profits of his Play which had been finished three Years*, and in another Letter declares his Resolution to publish a Pamphlet, that the World might know how *he had been used*.

This Pamphlet was never written, for he in a very short Time recover'd his usual Tranquillity, and chearfully applied himself to more inoffensive Studies. He indeed steadily declared, that he was promised a yearly Allowance of fifty Pounds, and never received half the Sum, but he seemed to resign himself to that as well as to other Misfortunes, and lose the Remembrance of it in his Amusements, and Employments.

The Chearfulness with which he bore his Confinement, appears from the following Letter which he wrote *Jan.* 30th, to one of his Friends in *London*.

I now write to you from my Confinement in *Newgate*, where I have been ever since Monday last was Sev'n-night; and where I enjoy myself with much more Tranquillity than I have known for upwards of a twelvemonth past; having a Room entirely to myself, and persuing the Amusement of my poetical Studies, uninterrupted and agreeable to my Mind. I thank the Almighty, I am now all collected in myself, and tho' my Person is in Confinement, my Mind can expatiate on ample and useful Subjects, with all the Freedom imaginable. I am now more conversant with the Nine than ever; and if, instead of a *Newgate* Bird, I may be allowed to be a Bird of the Muses, I assure you, Sir, I sing very freely in my Cage; sometimes indeed in the plaintive Notes of the Nightingale; but, at others, in the chearful Strains of the Lark.——

In another Letter he observes, that he ranges from one Subject to another without confining himself to any particular Task, and that he was employed one Week upon one Attempt, and the next upon another.

Surely the Fortitude of this Man deserves, at least, to be

mentioned with Applause, and whatever Faults may be imputed to him, the Virtue of *suffering well* cannot be denied him. The two Powers which, in the Opinion of *Epictetus*, constitute a wise Man, are those of *bearing* and *forbearing*, which cannot indeed be affirmed to have been equally possessed by *Savage*, but it was too manifest that the Want of one obliged him very *frequently* to practise the other.

He was treated by Mr *Dagg*, the Keeper of the Prison, with great Humanity; was supported by him at his own Table without any certainty of Recompense, had a Room to himself, to which he could at any Time retire from all Disturbance, was allowed to stand at the Door of the Prison, and sometimes taken out into the Fields; so that he suffered fewer Hardships in the Prison, than he had been accustomed to undergo in the greatest part of his Life.[93]

The Keeper did not confine his Benevolence to a gentle Execution of his Office, but made some Overtures to the Creditor for his Release, tho' without Effect; and continued, during the whole Time of his Imprisonment to treat him with the utmost Tenderness and Civility.

Virtue is undoubtedly most laudable in that State which makes it most difficult; and therefore the Humanity of a

[93] Abel Dagge was Keeper of Bristol Newgate Gaol, according to records of the Bristol Quarter Sessions in 1743. The name *Dagg* or *Dagge* turns up in the *Bristol Poll Books* through the century. What Johnson said about him is corroborated in two letters written by Savage: '. . . as I was standing at our door in the street (which I am allowed to do alone whenever I please), who should be passing by one evening but Mr. Becket? . . . In he came, and we drank in Mr. Dagge's parlour one negus and two pints of wine. . . . One day last week Mr. Dagge, finding me at the door, asked me to take a walk with him, which I did a mile beyond Baptist Mill in Gloucestershire; where, at a public-house, he treated me with ale and toddy. Baptist Mill is the pleasantest walk near this city. I found the smell of the new-mown hay very sweet, and every breeze was reviving to my spirits. . . . Mr. Price visits me in a friendly manner, and not long ago sent me a present of four pint-bottles of excellent rum, and two of as fine shrub, for punch. . . . I was yesterday, in the afternoon, out upon a field-walk again with Mr. Dagge, and we also regaled ourselves at a public-house in the city' (*GM.* 87. 1040–1).

Goaler, certainly deserves this publick Attestation; and the Man whose Heart has not been hardened by such an Employment, may be justly proposed as a Pattern of Benevolence. If an Inscription was once engraved to the *honest Toll-gatherer*, less Honours ought not to be paid *to the tender Goaler*.

Mr. *Savage* very frequently received Visits, and sometimes Presents from his Acquaintances, but they did not amount to a Subsistence, for the greater Part of which he was indebted to the Generosity of this Keeper; but these Favours, however they might endear to him the particular Persons, from whom he received them, were very far from impressing upon his Mind any advantageous Ideas of the People of *Bristol*, and therefore he thought he could not more properly employ himself in Prison, than in writing the following Poem.

LONDON *and* BRISTOL *delineated.*[94]

Two Sea-port Cities mark *Britannia*'s Fame,
And these from Commerce different Honours claim.
What different Honours shall the Muses pay,
While one inspires and one untunes the Lay?

---

* The Author preferr'd this Title to that *of* London *and* Bristol *compared*; which, when he began the Piece, he intended to prefix to it.

---

[94] This text, like that of *Volunteer Laureat*, no. 1, was cut out of 75 and 77b and all later editions. Though the words preceding it were modified accordingly, the reference in the sentence immediately following to 'the Chasm'—i.e. the hiatus in the poem—was left without meaning. Cf. p. 76 and n.

Cave must have retained the manuscript of this poem, which Savage had sent him from Bristol, because when Johnson announced in the newspapers his plan to write Savage's life, he mentioned his intention of including this poem. However, he was forestalled by M. Cooper, a bookseller, who got out an edition entitled *London and Bristol Compared* in December, just as Johnson was completing his work and receiving payment for it. Johnson's disappointment at being anticipated may partly account for the delay in publishing his Life.

The footnote added to the word '*delineated*' is, of course, Johnson's.

Now silver *Isis* bright'ning flows along,
Echoing from *Oxford*'s Shore each classic Song;
Then weds with *Tame*; and these, O *London*, see
Swelling with naval Pride, the Pride of Thee!
Wide deep unsullied *Thames* meand'ring glides
And bears thy Wealth on mild majestic Tides.
Thy Ships, with gilded Palaces that vie,
In glitt'ring Pomp, strike wond'ring *China*'s Eye;
And thence returning bear, in splendid State,
To *Britain*'s Merchants, *India*'s eastern Freight.
India, her Treasures from her western Shores,
Due at thy Feet, a willing Tribute pours;
Thy warring Navies distant Nations awe,
And bid the World obey thy righteous Law.
Thus shine thy manly Sons of lib'ral Mind;
Thy Change deep-busied, yet as Courts refin'd;
Councils, like Senates that enforce Debate
With fluent Eloquence and Reason's Weight.
Whose Patriot Virtue, lawless Pow'r controuls;
Their *British* emulating *Roman* Souls.
Of these the worthiest still selected stand,
Still lead the Senate, and still save the Land:
Social, not selfish, here, O Learning trace
Thy Friends, the Lovers of all human Race!

In a dark Bottom sunk, O *Bristol* now,
With native Malice, lift thy low'ring Brow!
Then as some Hell-born Sprite, in mortal Guise,
Borrows the Shape of Goodness and belies,
All fair, all smug to yon proud Hall invite,
To feast all Strangers ape an Air polite!
From *Cambria* drain'd, or *England*'s western Coast,
Not elegant yet costly Banquets boast!
Revere, or seem the Stranger to revere;
Praise, fawn, profess, be all Things but sincere;
Insidious now, our bosom Secrets steal,
And these with sly sarcastic Sneer reveal.
Present we meet thy sneaking treach'rous Smiles;

The harmless Absent still thy Sneer reviles;
Such as in Thee all Parts superior find;
The Sneer that marks the Fool and Knave combin'd.
When melting Pity wou'd afford Relief,
The ruthless Sneer that Insult adds to Grief.
What Friendship can'st thou boast? what Honours claim?
To Thee each Stranger owes an injur'd Name.
What Smiles thy Sons must in their Foes excite?
Thy Sons to whom all Discord is Delight;
From whom eternal mutual Railing flows;
Who in each others Crimes, their own expose;
Thy Sons, tho' crafty, deaf to Wisdom's Call;
Despising all Men and despis'd by all.
Sons, while thy Clifs a ditch-like River laves,
Rude as thy Rocks, and muddy as thy Waves;
Of Thoughts as narrow as of Words immense;
As full of Turbulence as void of Sense:
Thee, Thee what senatorial Souls adorn?
Thy Natives sure wou'd prove a Senate's Scorn.
Do Strangers deign to serve Thee? what their Praise?
Their gen'rous Services thy Murmurs raise.
What Fiend malign, that o'er thy Air presides,
Around from Breast to Breast inherent glides,
And, as he glides, there scatters in a Trice
The lurking Seeds of ev'ry rank Device?
Let foreign Youths to thy Indentures run!
Each, each will prove, in thy adopted Son,
Proud, pert and dull—Tho' brilliant once from Schools,
Will scorn all Learning's as all Virtue's Rules;
And, tho' by Nature friendly, honest, brave,
Turn a sly, selfish, simp'ring, sharping Knave.
Boast petty-Courts, where 'stead of fluent Ease;
Of cited Precedents and learned Pleas;
'Stead of sage Council in the dubious Cause,
Attorneys chatt'ring wild, burlesque the Laws.
So shameless Quacks, who Doctor's Rights invade,
Of Jargon and of Poison form a Trade.
So canting Coblers, while from Tubs they teach,

Buffoon the Gospel they pretend to preach.
Boast petty Courts, whence Rules new Rigour draw;
Unknown to Nature's and to Statute Law;
Quirks that explain all saving Rights away,
To give th' Attorney and the Catch-poll Prey.
Is there where Law too rig'rous may descend?
Or Charity her kindly Hand extend?
Thy Courts, that shut when Pity wou'd redress,
Spontaneous open to inflict Distress.
Try Misdemeanours!—all thy Wiles employ,
Not to chastise the Offender but destroy;
Bid the large lawless Fine his Fate foretell;
Bid it beyond his Crime and Fortune swell.
Cut off from Service due to kindred Blood
To private Welfare and to public Good,
Pitied by all, but thee, he sentenc'd lies,
Imprison'd languishes, imprison'd dies,

* * * * * * * * * * *
* * * * * * * * * * *
* * * * * * * * * * *
* * * * * * * * * * *
* * * * * * * * * * *
* * * * * * * * * * *

Boast swarming Vessels, whose *Plæbeian* State
Owes not to Merchants but Mechanics Freight.
Boast nought but Pedlar Fleets—In War's Alarms,
Unknown to Glory, as unknown to Arms.
Boast thy base * *Tolsey*, and thy turn-spit Dogs;
Thy † *Hallier*'s Horses and thy human Hogs;
Upstarts and Mushrooms, proud, relentless Hearts;
Thou Blank of Sciences! Thou Dearth of Arts!
Such Foes as Learning once was doom'd to see;
Huns, Goths, and *Vandals* were but Types of Thee.

* A Place where the Merchants used to meet to transact their Affairs before the Exchange was erected. *See Gentleman's Magazine.* Vol. xiii. p. 496.
† *Hallier*'s are the Persons who drive or own the Sledges, which are here used instead of Carts.

> Proceed, great *Bristol*, in all-righteous Ways
> And let one Justice heighten yet thy Praise;
> Still spare the Catamite and swinge the Whore,
> And be, whate'er *Gomorrah* was before.

When he had brought this Poem to its present State, which, without considering the Chasm, is not perfect, he wrote to *London* an Account of his Design, and informed his Friend,[95] that he was determined to print it with his Name; but enjoined him not to communicate his Intention to his *Bristol* Acquaintance. The Gentleman surprised at his Resolution, endeavoured to dissuade him from publishing it, at least, from prefixing his Name, and declared, that he could not reconcile the Injunction of Secrecy with his Resolution to own it at its first Appearance. To this Mr *Savage* returned an Answer agreeable to his Character in the following Terms.

I received yours this Morning and not without a little Surprize at the Contents. To answer a Question with a Question, you ask me concerning *London* and *Bristol*, *Why will I add* delineated? Why did Mr *Woolaston* add the same Word to his Religion of Nature? I suppose that it was his Will and Pleasure to add it in his Case; and it is mine to do so in my Own. You are pleased to tell me, that you understand not, why Secrecy is injoin'd, and yet I intend to set my Name to it. My Answer is—I have my private Reasons; which I am not obliged to explain to any One. You doubt, my Friend Mr S———[96] would not approve of it—And what is it to me whether he does or not? Do you imagine, that Mr S——— is to dictate to me? If any Man, who calls himself my Friend, should assume such an Air, I would spurn at his Friendship with Contempt. You say, I seem to think so by not letting him know it—And suppose

[95] Edward Cave, publisher of the *Gentleman's Magazine* (*GM.* 87. 1039 n.)

[96] Mr. Strong, an employee of the General Post Office in London, to whom in June 1743 Savage wrote two letters (*GM.* 87. 1039-41).

I do, what then? Perhaps I can give Reasons for that Disapprobation, very foreign from what you would imagine. You go on in saying, suppose, I should not put my Name to it—My Answer is, that I will not suppose any such Thing, being determined to the contrary; neither, Sir, would I have you suppose, that I applied to you for Want of another Press: Nor would I have you imagine, that I owe Mr S—— Obligations which I do not.

Such was his Imprudence and such his obstinate Adherence to his own Resolutions, however absurd. A Prisoner! supported by Charity! and, whatever Insults he might have received during the latter Part of his Stay in *Bristol*, once caressed, esteemed, and presented with a liberal Collection, he could forget on a sudden his Danger, and his Obligations, to gratify the Petulance of his Wit, or the Eagerness of his Resentment, and publish a Satire by which he might reasonably expect, that he should alienate those who then supported him, and provoke those whom he could neither resist nor escape.

This Resolution, from the Execution of which, it is probable, that only his Death could have hindered him, is sufficient to show, how much he disregarded all Considerations that opposed his present Passions, and how readily he hazarded all future Advantages for any immediate Gratifications. Whatever was his predominant Inclination, neither Hope nor Fear hinder'd him from complying with it, nor had Opposition any other Effect than to heighten his Ardour and irritate his Vehemence.

This Performance was however laid aside, while he was employed in soliciting Assistances from several great Persons, and one Interruption succeeding another hinder'd him from supplying the Chasm, and perhaps from retouching the other Parts, which he can hardly be imagined to have finished, in his own Opinion; for it is very unequal, and some of the Lines are rather inserted to rhyme to others than to support or improve the Sense; but the first and last Parts are worked up with great Spirit and Elegance.

His Time was spent in the Prison for the most part in Study, or in receiving Visits; but sometimes he descended to lower Amusements, and diverted himself in the Kitchen with the Conversation of the Criminals[97]; for it was not pleasing to him to be much without Company, and though he was very capable of a judicious Choice, he was often contented with the first that offered; for this he was sometimes reproved by his Friends who found him surrounded with Felons; but the Reproof was on that as on other Occasions thrown away; he continued to gratify himself, and to set very little Value on the Opinion of others.

But here, as in every other Scene of his Life, he made use of such Opportunities as occur'd of benefiting those who were more miserable than himself, and was always ready to perform any Offices of Humanity to his fellow Prisoners.

He had now ceased from corresponding with any of his Subscribers except one,[98] who yet continued to remit him the twenty Pounds a Year which he had promised him, and by whom it was expected, that he would have been in a very short Time enlarged, because he had directed the Keeper to enquire after the State of his Debts.

However he took Care to enter his Name according to the Forms of the Court, that the Creditor might be obliged to make him some Allowance, if he was continued a Prisoner, and when on that Occasion he appeared in the Hall was treated with very unusual Respect.[99]

[97] In the left-hand margin opposite this sentence in the Euing copy Johnson wrote: 'Saunders'. Probably he was noting the source of his information.

[98] In the margin opposite this sentence in the Euing copy Johnson wrote: 'Pope'.

[99] In the margin opposite this sentence in the Euing copy Johnson wrote: 'Pope's letter in his Life by Roughead'. Cf. *Correspondence of Pope*, iv. 392–3, 417–18. On 19 June 1743 Savage wrote as follows to Mr. Strong: 'As for Madam Wolf Bitch [i.e. Mrs. Read], the African monster,

But the Resentment of the City was afterwards raised by some Accounts that had been spread of the Satire, and he was informed that some of the Merchants intended to pay the Allowance which the Law required, and to detain him Prisoner at their own Expence. This he treated as an empty Menace, and perhaps might have hasten'd the Publication, only to shew how much he was superior to their Insults, had not all his Schemes been suddenly destroyed.

When he had been six Months in Prison he received from one of his Friends*[100] in whose Kindness he had the greatest

* Mr. *Pope*.

Mr. Dagge, unknown to me, offered her . . . three guineas to release me. She asked time to consider of it; and . . . sent him word, that she was determined to keep me in confinement a twelvemonth: however, she will soon be perhaps sick of her resolution. Through Mr. Ward's means I was last court-day but one sent for up by *habeas corpus* to the Guildhall, where a rule, on my appearance there, was entered, to force her to proceed to execution; which if she does not by the next court-day, her action will be superseded; and if she does, then Madam Wolf Bitch must allow the two shillings and four pence per week. . . . [Mr. Becket] told me, the city were highly exasperated at my Satire, and that some of the merchants would, by way of revenge, subscribe the two and four pence to confine me still. But this I looked on as bravado, and treated it with contempt. . . . When I appeared at the Guildhall, the Court paid me great deference and respect' (*GM*. 87. 1040). Savage appeared before the Tolsey Court on Monday, 30 May 1743, 'upon precept of habeas corpus', and the plaintiff was ordered 'to enter up his [her] judgment . . . otherwise he shall be discharged on filing common bail by consent'. On 27 June the plaintiff did enter up her judgement and prayed the defendant 'in execution' [=custody] (Rule Book of the Tolsey Court).

[100] The footnote here was not added until 1775, but in the margin opposite these words in the Euing copy of 48 Johnson wrote: 'Pope', and at the foot of the page added, with obvious reference to this passage: 'Henly. P——'s treatment of Savage.' In the last edition published during his lifetime, that of 1783, he added the following sentences in the text after the word 'dictated': 'Henley, in one of his advertisements, had mentioned *Pope's treatment of Savage*. This was supposed by Pope to be the consequence of a complaint made by Savage to Henley, and was therefore mentioned by him with much resentment.' Johnson had evidently forgotten that he had not previously mentioned Pope's name in this connection and so could not have realized that the unexplained intrusion of it here would only puzzle the reader. Consequently I have omitted the passage, even though it clearly has Johnson's authorization.

Pope's letter has not come to light. Professor Sherburn believed that the severe one dated by Elwin and Courthope in 1743 was actually written

Confidence, and on whose Assistance he chiefly depended, a Letter that contained a Charge of very atrocious Ingratitude, drawn up in such Terms as sudden Resentment dictated. Mr *Savage* returned a very solemn Protestation of his Innocence, but however appeared much disturbed at the Accusation. Some Days afterwards he was seized with a Pain in his Back and Side, which as it was not violent was not suspected to be dangerous; but growing daily more languid and dejected, on the 25th of *July* he confined himself to his Room, and a Fever seized his Spirits. The Symptoms grew every Day more formidable, but his Condition did not enable him to procure any Assistance. The last Time that the Keeper saw him was on *July* the 31st, 1743; when *Savage* seeing him at his Bed-side said, with an uncommon Earnestness, *I have something to say to you, Sir*, but after a Pause, moved his Hand in a melancholy Manner, and finding himself unable to recollect what he was going to communicate, said *'Tis gone*. The Keeper soon after left him, and the next Morning he died.[101] He was buried in the Church-yard of St *Peter*, at the Expence of the Keeper.

Such were the Life and Death of *Richard Savage*, a Man equally distinguished by his Virtues and Vices, and at once remarkable for his Weaknesses and Abilities.

He was of a middle Stature, of a thin Habit of Body, a long Visage, coarse Features, and melancholy Aspect; of a grave and manly Deportment, a solemn Dignity of Mien, but which upon a nearer Acquaintance softened into an

in 1742, before Savage went to prison (*Correspondence of Pope*, iv. 392). If so, it cannot have been the one referred to here. Johnson alluded to it again in his 'Repertorium', written *c*. 31 Oct. 1784. *Diaries, Prayers, and Annals*, ed. E. L. McAdam *et al.* (New Haven, 1958), p. 408.

'Orator' Henley was a mountebank preacher who raked up as much muck as he could and who used to advertise the topics of his sermons in the newspapers.

[101] The *Gentleman's Magazine* gave the date of Savage's death as 5 Aug., but Johnson's date—1 Aug.—must be correct, because the burial was registered at the Church of St. Peter, Bristol, under date of 2 Aug. (*Notes and Queries*, 2nd Ser. iv (1857), 286).

engaging Easiness of Manners. His Walk was slow, and his Voice tremulous and mournful. He was easily excited to Smiles, but very seldom provoked to Laughter.

His Mind was in an uncommon Degree vigorous and active. His Judgment was accurate, his Apprehension quick, and his Memory so tenacious, that he was frequently observed to know what he had learned from others in a short Time better than those by whom he was informed, and could frequently recollect Incidents, with all their Combination of Circumstances, which few would have regarded at the present Time; but which the Quickness of his Apprehension impressed upon him. He had the peculiar Felicity, that his Attention never deserted him; he was present to every Object, and regardful of the most trifling Occurrences. He had the Art of escaping from his own Reflections and accomodating himself to every new Scene.

To this Quality is to be imputed the Extent of his Knowledge compared with the small Time which he spent in visible Endeavours to acquire it. He mingled in cursory Conversation with the same Steadiness of Attention as others apply to a Lecture, and, amidst the Appearance of thoughtless Gayety, lost no new Idea that was started, nor any Hint that could be improved. He had therefore made in Coffee-houses the same Proficiency as others in their Closets; and it is remarkable, that the Writings of a Man of little Education and little Reading have an Air of Learning scarcely to be found in any other Performances, but which perhaps as often obscures as embellishes them.

His Judgment was eminently exact both with regard to Writings and to Men. The Knowledge of Life was indeed his chief Attainment, and it is not without some Satisfaction, that I can produce the Suffrage of *Savage* in favour of human Nature, of which he never appeared to entertain such odious Ideas, as some who perhaps had neither his Judgment nor Experience have published, either in Ostenta-

tion of their Sagacity, Vindication of their Crimes, or Gratification of their Malice.

His Method of Life particularly qualified him for Conversation, of which he knew how to practise all the Graces.
He was never vehement or loud, but at once modest and
easy, open and respectful, his Language was vivacious and
elegant, and equally happy upon grave or humorous Subjects. He was generally censured for not knowing when to
retire, but that was not the Defect of his Judgment, but of
his Fortune; when he left his Company he was frequently
to spend the remaining Part of the Night in the Street, or
at least was abandoned to gloomy Reflections, which it
is not strange that he delayed as long as he could, and
sometimes forgot that he gave others Pain to avoid it
himself.

It cannot be said, that he made Use of his Abilities for the
Direction of his own Conduct; an irregular and dissipated
Manner of Life had made him the Slave of every Passion
that happened to be excited by the Presence of its Object,
and that Slavery to his Passions reciprocally produced a
Life irregular and dissipated.[102] He was not Master of his
own Motions, nor could promise any Thing for the
next Day.

With Regard to his Oeconomy, nothing can be added
to the Relation of his Life: he appeared to think himself
born to be supported by others, and dispensed from all
Necessity of providing for himself; he therefore never
prosecuted any Scheme of Advantage, nor endeavoured
even to secure the Profits which his Writings might have
afforded him.

His Temper was in consequence of the Dominion of his
Passions uncertain and capricious; he was easily engaged,

---

[102] To dissipate was 'to scatter the attention' (Johnson's *Dictionary*,
where a part of this sentence is quoted). It did not imply licentiousness;
cf. p. 104.

and easily disgusted; but he is accused of retaining his Hatred more tenaciously than his Benevolence.

He was compassionate both by Nature and Principle, and always ready to perform Offices of Humanity; but when he was provoked, and very small Offences were sufficient to provoke him, he would prosecute his Revenge with the utmost Acrimony till his Passion had subsided.

His Friendship was therefore of little Value; for though he was zealous in the Support or Vindication of those whom he loved, yet it was always dangerous to trust him, because he considered himself discharged by the first Quarrel, from all Ties of Honour or Gratitude; and would betray those Secrets which in the Warmth of Confidence had been imparted to him. This Practice drew upon him an universal Accusation of Ingratitude; nor can it be denied that he was very ready to set himself free from the Load of an Obligation; for he could not bear to conceive himself in a State of Dependence, his Pride being equally powerful with his other Passions, and appearing in the Form of Insolence at one time and of Vanity at another. Vanity the most innocent Species of Pride, was most frequently predominant: he could not easily leave off when he had once begun to mention himself or his Works, nor ever read his Verses without stealing his Eyes from the Page, to discover in the Faces of his Audience, how they were affected with any favourite Passage.

A kinder Name than that of Vanity ought to be given to the Delicacy with which he was always careful to separate his own Merit from every other Man's; and to reject that Praise to which he had no Claim. He did not forget, in mentioning his Performances, to mark every Line that had been suggested or amended, and was so accurate as to relate that he owed *three Words* in THE WANDERER, to the Advice of his Friends.

His Veracity was questioned but with little reason; his

Accounts, tho' not indeed always the same, were generally consistent. When he loved any Man, he suppress'd all his Faults, and when he had been offended by him, concealed all his Virtues: but his Characters were generally true, so far as he proceeded; tho' it cannot be denied that his Partiality might have sometimes the Effect of Falsehood.

In Cases indifferent he was zealous for Virtue, Truth and Justice; he knew very well the Necessity of Goodness to the present and future Happiness of Mankind; nor is there perhaps any Writer, who has less endeavoured to please by flattering the Appetites or perverting the Judgment.

As an Author, therefore, and he now ceases to influence Mankind in any other Character, if one Piece which he had resolved to suppress be excepted, he has very little to fear from the strictest moral or religious Censure. And though he may not be altogether secure against the Objections of the Critic, it must however be acknowledged, that his Works are the Productions of a Genius truly poetical; and, what many Writers who have been more lavishly applauded cannot boast, that they have an original Air, which has no Resemblance of any foregoing Work; that the Versification and Sentiments have a Cast peculiar to themselves, which no Man can imitate with Success, because what was Nature in *Savage* would in another be Affectation. It must be confessed that his Descriptions are striking, his Images animated, his Fictions justly imagined, and his Allegories artfully persued; that his Diction is elevated, though sometimes forced, and his Numbers sonorous and majestick, though frequently sluggish and encumbered. Of his Stile the general Fault is Harshness, and the general Excellence is Dignity; of his Sentiments the prevailing Beauty is Sublimity, and Uniformity the prevailing Defect.

For his Life, or for his Writings, none who candidly consider his Fortune, will think an Apology either necessary or difficult. If he was not always sufficiently instructed in his

Subject, his Knowledge was at least greater than could have been attained by others in the same State. If his Works were sometimes unfinished, Accuracy cannot reasonably be exacted from a Man oppressed with Want, which he has no Hope of relieving but by a speedy Publication. The Insolence and Resentment of which he is accused, were not easily to be avoided by a great Mind, irritated by perpetual Hardships and constrained hourly to return the Spurns of Contempt, and repress the Insolence of Prosperity; and Vanity surely may be readily pardoned in him, to whom Life afforded no other Comforts than barren Praises, and the Consciousness of deserving them.

Those are no proper Judges of his Conduct who have slumber'd away their Time on the Down of Plenty, nor will a wise Man easily presume to say, 'Had I been in *Savage*'s Condition, I should have lived, or written, better than *Savage*.'

This[103] Relation will not be wholly without its Use, if those, who languish under any Part of his Sufferings, shall be enabled to fortify their Patience by reflecting that they feel only those Afflictions from which the Abilities of *Savage* did not exempt him; or if those, who in Confidence of superior Capacities or Attainments disregard the common Maxims of Life, shall be reminded that nothing will supply the Want of Prudence, and that Negligence and Irregularity, long continued, will make Knowledge useless, Wit ridiculous, and Genius contemptible.

FINIS.

---

[103] In the margin opposite the beginning of this final paragraph in the Euing copy Johnson wrote: 'Added'.

TEXTUAL NOTES

Symbols:

C= *A Collection of Pieces in Verse and Prose, Which have been Published on Occasion of the DUNCIAD,* 1732.

GM= *Gentleman's Magazine.* (Reference is made in this way: *GM.* 53. 491=page 491 of the volume for 1753.)

MP= *Miscellaneous Poems and Translations.* By Several Hands. Publish'd by Richard Savage. 1726.

ms.= Manuscript notes in Johnson's hand in the copy of the *Life* in the Euing Collection in Glasgow University Library.

PS= *Of Public Spirit in Regard to Public Works,* 1739.

STO=*The Tragedy of Sir Thomas Overbury,* 1724.

W= *The Wanderer: A Poem.* 1729.

WM= *Weekly Miscellany,* 3 April 1735.

Editions of Johnson's *Life* are designated by the last two digits of their dates, as shown in the TEXTUAL INTRODUCTION.

3. 1–3	*Title*] 44, 48, 67, 77a; DR. JOHNSON'S LIFE OF THE AUTHOR. 75, 77b; SAVAGE. 79–81, 81, 83.
3. 7	Station.] 44, 48, 67, 75, 77a, 77b, 79–81; Station: 81, 83.
3. 11	drew] 44, 48, 75, 77b, 79–81, 81, 83; draw 67, 77a.
3. 11	them universal] ms.; them an universal 44, 48, 67, 75, 77a, 77b, 79–81, 81, 83.
3. 15	extrinsic] 44, 48, 67, 75, 77b, 79–81, 81, 83; intrinsic 77a.
3. 18	Expectation] 48, 67, 77a; Expectations 44, 75, 77b, 79–81, 81, 83.
4. 4	suffered, than for what they have] 44, 48, 67, 75, 77a, 77b; *omitted* 79–81, 81, 83.
4. 14	*Macclesfield,*] 48, 67, 75, 77a, 77b, 79–81, 81, 83; *Macclesfield* 44.

4. 19–20   Her Husband, being as] ms.; This, as 44, 75, 77b, 79–81, 81, 83; Her Husband, as 48, 67, 77a.

4. 20   imagined, thus made] ms.; imagined, made her Husband 44, 75, 77b, 79–81, 81, 83; imagined, being thus made 48, 67, 77a.

4. 21   prosecuted] 48, 67, 77a; and he prosecuted 44, 75, 77b, 79–81, 81, 83.

4. 25   Child] 48, 67, 77a; Children 44, 75, 77b, 79–81, 81, 83.

5. 3   next year] ms.; *omitted* 44, 48, 67, 75, 77a, 77b, 79–81, 81, 83.

5. 3   *March* 3d] 44, 48, 75, 77b, 79–81, 81, 83; *March* the 3d, 67, 77a.

5. 5   having, as well as her Husband, the] ms., 67, 75, 77a, 77b, 79–81, 81, 83; having as well as her Husband the 44, 48.

6. 8   incited] 44, 48, 67, 75, 77b, 79–81, 81, 83; inclined 77a.

6. 10   Crimes] 44, 48, 67, 75, 77a, 79–81, 81, 83; Crime 77b.

6. 12   that] 48, 67, 77a; which 44, 75, 77b, 79–81, 81, 83.

6. 18   Misery; that] ms.; Misery, or that 44, 75, 77b, 79–81, 81, 83; Misery, that 48, 67, 77a.

6. 30   Riches] 48, 67, 77a; Affluence 44, 75, 77b, 79–81, 81, 83.

7. 7   his Nurse] 48, 67, 77a; the Nurse 44, 75, 77b, 79–81, 81, 83.

7. 7   pay] 48, 67, 77a; to pay 44, 75, 77b, 79–81, 81, 83.

7. 7   superintend] 48, 67, 77a; to superintend 44, 75, 77b, 79–81, 81, 83.

7. 7–8   his Education] 48, 67, 77a; the Education of the Child 44, 75, 77b, 79–81, 81, 83.

7. 16   Claim, or] ms.; Claim, to shelter him from Oppression, or 44, 48, 67, 75, 77a, 77b, 79–81, 81, 83.

8. 10   There is reason] ms.; It is very reasonable 44, 48, 67, 75, 77a, 77b, 79–81, 81, 83.

8. 13   early] ms.; earliest 44, 48, 67, 75, 77a, 77b, 79–81, 81, 83.

8. 15   Sallies] ms.; vigorous Sallies 44, 48, 67, 75, 77a, 77b, 79–81, 81, 83.

8. 17   Touches of that vigorous] ms.; strong Touches of that ardent 44, 48, 67, 75, 77a, 77b, 79–81, 81, 83.

8. 19   Mind] ms.; Genius 44, 48, 67, 75, 77a, 77b, 79–81, 81, 83.

9. 8   in a human] 44, 48, 75, 77b, 79–81, 81, 83; in human 67, 77a.

9. 15   to a] ms.; a 44, 48, 67, 75, 77a, 77b, 79–81, 81, 83.

10. 1   even those] 48, 67, 77a; those 44, 75, 77b, 79–81, 81, 83.

10. 23 take] 44, 48, 67, 75, 77a, 79–81, 81, 83; *omitted* 77b.

10. 24 *Preface to *Savage*'s Miscellanies.] 44, 75, 77b, 79–81, 81, 83; *combined with previous footnote,* 48; *omitted* 67, 77a.

11. 7   now] 44, 48, 67, 75, 77a, 77b, 79–81; *omitted* 81, 83.

11. 14 upon her] 48, 67, 77a; upon her Mind 44, 75, 77b, 79–81, 81, 83.

12. 14 of] 44, 48, 75, 77b, 79–81, 81, 83; for 67, 77a.

12. 27 that] 44, 48, 67, 75, 77a, 79–81, 81, 83; *omitted* 77b.

12. 29 *Plain Dealer.] 48, 67, 77a; *Plain Dealer. See Appendix. 44, 75, 77b; *See the PLAIN DEALER. 79–81, 81, 83.

13. 9   this] 48, 67, 77a; his 44, 75, 77b, 79–81, 81, 83.

13. 20–1 all Opportunities] 44, 48, 67, 75, 77a, 77b; all the opportunities 79–81, 81, 83.

14. 11–12 his Friend] 48, 67, 77a; Sir *Richard* 44, 75, 77b, 79–81, 81, 83.

14. 16 had desired] 44, 48, 75, 77b, 79–81, 81, 83; desired 67, 77a.

14. 18 Work,] 44, 48, 67, 77a; Work. 75, 77b, 79–81, 81, 83.

15. 15   He with great Frankness] 48, 67, 77a; Sir *Richard*
          very frankly 44, 75, 77b, 79–81, 81, 83.

15. 17   that] 44, 48, 67, 75, 77b, 79–81, 81, 83; *omitted* 77a.

17. 7   State] 44, 48, 67, 77a; case 75, 77b, 79–81, 81, 83.

17. 29   was] 75, 77b, 79–81, 81, 83; is now 44, 48, 67, 77a.

18. 24   published 1727] 44, 48, 75, 77b, 79–81, 81, 83; pub-
          lished in 1727 67, 77a.

20. 29   it] 44, 48, 67, 75, 77a, 77b, 79–81; him 81, 83.

21. 24   he] 48, 67, 77a, 77b, 79–81, 81, 83; his 44, 75.

21. 27   or] 44, 48, 75, 77b, 79–81, 81, 83; and 67, 77a.

21. 27   Streets] 48, 67, 77a; Street 44, 75 77b, 79–81, 81, 83.

22. 5   ingenuous] 44, 48, 67, 75, 77a, 79–81, 81, 83; ingenious
          77b.

22. 15 ff.   *footnote*] 44, 48, 67, 77a; *replaced by* Vol. II p. 181.
          75, 77b; *omitted* 79–81, 81, 83.

22. 19   instruct] 44, 48, 67, 77a; excel *MP*.

22. 20   whom] 44, 48, 67, 77a; thee *MP*.

22. 27   sooths] 44, 48, 67, 77a; charms *MP*.

23. 16 ff.   *footnote*] 44, 48, 67, 77a; *replaced by* Ibid, p. 150.
          75, 77b; *replaced by* Printed in this Volume. 79–81;
          replaced by Printed in the late colection of his
          poems. 81, 83.

23. 19   Shews] 44, 48, 67, 77a; Grows *MP*.

23. 28   and] 44, 48, 67, 77a; or *MP*.

23. 30 ff.   *footnote*] 44, 48, 67, 77a; *replaced by* Vol. I. p. 148,
          186. 75, 77b; *replaced by* See Savage's Works, vol.
          I. p. 148. 186. 79–81; *omitted* 81, 83.

23. 31   by] 44, 48, 67, 77a; of *STO*.

24. 5   Mr.] 44, 48, 67, 75, 77a, 77b, 81, 83; of Mr. 79–81.

24. 5   Part of] 44, 48, 67, 75, 77a, 77b, 81, 83; Part 79–81.

24. 9   are expected] 44, 48, 67, 75, 77a, 77b; were expected
          79–81, 81, 83.

24. 10   himself] 44, 48, 67, 75, 77a, 77b; *omitted* 79–81, 81, 83.

24. 16   Poverty] 48, 67, 77a; Poverty and *Cibber* 44, 75, 77b, 79–81, 81, 83.

24. 30   ¶] 44, 48, 67, 77a; *run together* 75, 77b, 79–81, 81, 83.

24. 31   *To *Herbert Tryst,* Esq; of *Herefordshire.*] 79–81, 81, 83; *To —— *Tryste,* Esq; of *Herefordshire.* 44, 48, 67, 77a; *To Herbert Tryst, Esq; of Herefordshire, vol. I. p. 111. 75, 77b.

25. 13 ff.   *footnote*] 44, 48, 67, 75, 77a, 77b; *omitted* 79–81, 81, 83.

27. 1   publish'd] 48, 67, 77a; wrote 44, 75, 77b, 79–81, 81, 83.

27. 6 ff.   *footnote*] 44, 48, 67, 75, 77a, 77b; *omitted* 79–81, 81, 83.

27. 27   the *Levitical*] *MP*; *Levitical* 44, 48, 67, 75, 77a, 77b.

27. 30   *on*] *MP*; *upon* 44, 48, 67, 75, 77a, 77b.

27. 37   came] *MP*; am 44, 48, 67, 75, 77a, 77b.

27. 39   now] *MP*; not 44, 48, 67, 75, 77a, 77b.

27. 44   stranger]*MP*, 44, 75, 77b; stronger 48, 67, 77a.

28. 18–19 By means of which natural Defect,] *MP*; *omitted* 44, 48, 67, 75, 77a, 77b.

28. 41   follows] *MP*; follow 44, 48, 67, 75, 77a, 77b.

28. 45   grow] *MP*; be 44, 48, 67, 75, 77a, 77b.

29. 13   but] *MP*; *omitted* 44, 48, 67, 75, 77a, 77b.

29. 17   had] *MP*; *omitted* 44, 48, 67, 75, 77a, 77b.

29. 38   with] 44, 48, 67, 75, 77a, 77b, 79–81, 81, 83; by *MP*.

29. 43–4 Force and Grace] 44, 48, 67, 75, 77a, 77b, 79–81, 81, 83; Grace and Force *MP*.

29. 45   and in] 44, 48, 67, 75, 77a, 77b, 79–81, 81, 83; and *MP*.

31. 13   their] 44, 48, 67, 75, 77a, 77b, 79–81; this 81, 83.

31. 13   Light] 44, 48, 67, 75, 77a, 77b; a light 79–81, 81, 83.

33. 7   Quarrel] 48, 67, 77a; Dispute 44, 75, 77b, 79–81, 81, 83.

33. 25   his Escape] 44, 48, 67, 77a; to escape 75, 77b, 79–81, 81, 83.

34. 15   had summed] 44, 48, 75, 77b, 79–81, 81, 83; summed 67, 77a.

35. 28   ought] 44, 48, 67, 75, 77a, 77b; *omitted* 79–81, 81, 83.

36. 8   a] 44, 48, 67, 77a; *omitted* 75, 77b, 79–81, 81, 83.

37. 3   none] 48, 67; no Persons 44, 75, 77b; nobody 77a; no person 79–81, 81, 83.

37. 23   Treatments] 44, 48, 67, 75, 77a, 77b; treatment 79–81, 81, 83.

38. 22   prosecute] 48, 67, 77a, 81, 83; persecute 44, 75, 77b, 79–81.

38. 23   Arts] 79–81, 81, 83; Acts 44, 48, 67, 75, 77a, 77b.

39. 7   alive*/*Anno* 1743.] 67, 77a; alive 44, 48, 75, 77b, 79–81, 81, 83.

39. 21   an] 44, 48, 75, 77b, 79–81, 81, 83; *omitted* 67, 77a.

40. 9   Women] 44, 48, 67, 75, 77a, 79–81; woman 77b, 81, 83.

40. 12   had] 44, 48, 67, 75, 77b, 79–81, 81, 83; he had 77a.

40. 29   any] 44, 48, 67, 75, 77a, 79–81, 81, 83; an 77b.

41. 14 ff.   *footnote*] 44, 48, 67, 77a; *replaced by* Vol. II. p. 208. 75, 77b; *replaced by* Printed in this Volume. 79–81; *replaced by* Printed in the late collection. 81, 83.

41. 14   The Satire] 44, 48; This Satire 67, 77a.

41. 25   Cases] *GM.* 41. 494; Causes 44, 48, 67, 77a.

42. 29 ff.   *footnote*] 44, 48, 67, 77a; *replaced by* Vol. II. p. 93. 75, 77b; *omitted* 79–81, 81, 83.

42. 34   *thou*] *GM.* 37. 113; then 44, 48, 67, 77a.

42. 43   perhaps] *GM.* 37. 113, 44; one Day 48, 67, 77a.

42. 46   *Bastard*] 44, 48; *The* BASTARD. 67, 77a.

43. 1   Occasion] 44, 48, 75, 77b, 79–81, 81, 83; the Occasion 67, 77a.

43. 21   habituated] 44, 48, 67, 75, 77a, 77b, 79–81; habituating 81, 83.

44. 2   was as] 44, 48, 75, 77b, 79–81, 81, 83; always 67, 77a.

45. 17   *let*] 44, 48, 67, 77a; LET*/*Vol. II. p. 231. 75; LET*/*Vol. II. p. 237. 77b; LET*/*Printed in his Works, vol. II. p. 231, 79–81, 81, 83.

46. 3   nearly] 44, 48, 67, 75, 77a, 77b; narrowly 79–81, 81, 83.

46. 27   The] 67, 77a; If the 44, 48, 75, 77b, 79–81, 81, 83.

46. 31 ff. *footnote*] 44, 48, 67, 77a; *replaced by* Vol. II. p. 233. 75; *replaced by* Vol. II. p. 239. 77b; *replaced by* See his Works, vol. II. p. 233. 79–81, 81, 83.

46. 35   may] *C*; will 44, 48, 67, 77a.

47. 15   purely by an] *C*, 44, 48; merely by 67, 77a.

48. 2–3 Satisfaction. [*New paragraph.*] The] 44, 48, 67, 77a; satisfaction; the 75, 77b, 79–81, 81, 83.

48. 10   License] *C*; Liberty 44, 48, 67, 77a.

48. 12   this with] *C*, 44, 48, 67; with this 77a.

48. 42   and] *C*, 44, 48, 67; *omitted* 77a.

48. 43   bought] *C*, 67, 77a; brought 44, 48.

49. 6   satirised] 44, 48, 67, 75, 77a, 77b, 81, 83; satisfied 79–81.

49. 24   also] *C*, 44; *omitted* 48, 67, 77a.

51. 11   Wealth] 48, 67, 77a; Affluence 44, 75, 77b, 79–81, 81, 83.

51. 24   the] 44, 48, 75, 77b, 79–81, 81, 83; *omitted* 67, 77a.

51. 27   Menaces] 44, 48, 75, 77b, 79–81, 81, 83; Menace 67, 77a.

52. 13–14 Consequence] 48, 67, 77a; Consequences 44, 75, 77b, 79–81, 81, 83.

52. 17   supported] 48, 67, 77a; surrounded 44, 75, 77b, 79–81, 81, 83.

52. 20   I fly] 44, 48, 67, 75, 77a, 77b, 79–81, 81, 83; She flies *W*.

53. 2   was asked] 67, 77a; asked 44, 48, 75, 77b, 79–81, 81, 83.

53. 16   Opinion; he] 48, 67, 77a; Opinion, and 44, 75, 77b, 79–81, 81, 83.

53. 30 ff. *footnote*] 44, 48, 67, 77a; *replaced by* Vol. II. p. 41. 75, 77b; *omitted* 79–81, 81, 83.

53. 32   these] 44, 48, 67, 77a; those *W*.

53. 33   should] 44, 48, 67, 77a; shall *W*.

54. 2   made] 44, 48, 67, 77a; *omitted* 75, 77b, 79–81, 81, 83.

54. 15   his] 44, 48, 67, 77a; the *W*.

54. 18   grow] 44, 48, 67, 77a; grew *W*.

54. 19 ff. *footnote*] 44, 48, 67, 77a; *replaced by* Vol. II. p. 59. 75, 77b; *omitted* 79–81, 81, 83.

54. 27   well] *W*, 44; swell 48, 67, 77a.

54. 33   nether] *W*, 44, 48; neither 67, 77a.

55. 3   suffer] 44, 48, 67, 75, 77a, 77b, 79–81; suffered 81, 83.

55. 8   Prospect] *W*, 44; Prospects 48, 67, 77a.

55. 12 ff. *footnote*] 44, 48, 67, 77a; *replaced by* Ibid. p. 27. 75, 77b; *omitted* 79–81, 81, 83.

55. 36   that] *W*, 44, 48; the 67, 77a.

56. 4   Eye] *W*; Eyes 44, 48, 67, 77a.

56. 1   Mr.] 44, 75, 77b, 79–81, 81, 83; *omitted* 48, 67, 77a.

56. 5   purpled] *W*, 44, 48; purple 67, 77a.

56. 6   Then] *W*; She 44, 48, 67, 77a.

56. 10 ff. *footnote*] 44, 48, 67, 77a; *replaced by* Ibid. p. 73. 75, 77b; *omitted* 79–81, 81, 83.

56. 10   *His*] 48, 67, 77a; *These* 44.

56. 20   Rod] *W*, 48, 67, 77a; Road 44.

56. 26   tho'] *W*; and 44, 48, 67, 77a.

57. 25   Sculpture] *W*, 44, 48; Sculptor 67, 77a.

58. 26   Perplexities; he] 44, 48, 67, 75, 77a, 77b, 79–81; per-
          plexities. He 81, 83.

58. 29   perhaps] 48, 67, 77a; and perhaps 44, 75, 77b, 79–81,
          81, 83.

58. 32   rig'rous] *W*, 48, 67, 77a; vig'rous 44.

59. 20   Companions 48, 67, 77a; Company 44, 75, 77b, 79–81,
          81, 83.

59. 26 ff. *footnote*] 44, 48, 67, 77a; *replaced by* Vol. II. p. 7. 75,
          77b; *omitted* 79–81, 81, 83.

59. 30   Thy] 44, 48, 67, 77a; That *W*.

59. 34   While] 44, 48, 67, 77a; When *W*.

60. 20   his Reckoning] 44, 48, 67, 75, 77a, 77b, 79–81; the
          reckoning 81, 83.

60. 32   would not] 44 (*erratum notice*) 48, 67, 77a; would
          44, 75, 77b, 79–81, 81, 83.

60. 33   *T——l*] 44, 48, 67, 75, 77a, 77b, 79–81; Tyrconnel
          81, 83.

61. 15   even] 48, 67, 77a; *omitted* 44, 75, 77b, 79–81, 81, 83.

61. 29 ff. *footnote*] 44, 48, 67, 77a; *replaced by* Vol. II. p. 3. 75,
          77b; *omitted* 79–81, 81, 83.

61. 32–3 Goodness and Generosity, which] 44, 48, 67, 77a;
          Goodness, the Generosity of which *W*.

61. 33   lately] 44, 48, 67, 77a; greatly *W*.

62. 12   upon] 44, 48, 67, 77a; on *W*.

62. 18   to] 44, 48, 67, 77a; into *W*.

62. 24   should] 44, 48, 67, 77a; shall *W*.

62. 27 ff. *footnote*] 44, 48, 67, 77a; *replaced by* Vol. II. p. 99.
          75, 77b; *omitted* 79–81, 81, 83.

62. 31   loving] *GM*. 37. 243, 48, 67, 77a; living 44.

62. 36   and] 44, 48, 67, 77a; Love, *GM*. 37. 243.

62. 38 Gay talk] *GM*. 37. 243; gay Talk 44, 48, 67, 77a.

63. 1–2 the Ideas] 44, 48, 75, 77b, 79–81, 81, 83; Ideas 67, 77a.

63. 16 Source] 44, 48, 67, 77a; life *GM*. 37. 243.

63. 25 a Mountain's Brow] 44, 48, 67, 77a; the mountain-brow *GM*. 37. 243.

63. 26 earliest] *GM*. 37. 243, 44, 48, 67, earlier 77a.

63. 30 Thereof] 44, 48, 67, 77a; There oft *GM*. 37. 243.

63. 31 Breath] 44, 48, 67, 77a; gale *GM*. 37. 243.

63. 42 *footnote*] 48; *replaced by* See the whole poem in the *Gentleman's Magazine*, Vol. VII, p. 243, 67, 77a; *omitted* 44, 75, 77b, 79–81, 81, 83.

65. 25 was now] 44, 48, 75, 77b, 79–81, 81, 83; are now 67, 77a.

66. 3 suspected] 44, 48, 75, 77b, 79–81, 81, 83; expected 67, 77a.

66. 16 which he] 44, 48, 67, 77a; he 75, 77b, 79–81, 81, 83.

68. 23 him] 44, 48, 67, 75, 77a, 79–81, 81, 83; *omitted* 77b.

69. 4–5 suffer themselves] 48, 67, 77a; suffered himself 44, 75, 77b, 79–81, 81, 83.

70. 11 enjoy] 44, 48, 75, 77b, 79–81, 81, 83; endure 67, 77a.

70. 17 ff. *footnote*] 44, 48, 67, 77a; *replaced by* Vol. II. p. 91. 75, 77b; *replaced by* Reprinted in this volume. 79–81; *omitted* 81, 83.

70. 22 with] 44, 48, 67, 77a; of *GM*. 37. 113.

71. 30 uninspir'd] 44, 48, 67, 77a; misinspired *GM*. 37. 113.

71. 36 Sinclair] 44, 48; *Mr*. Sinclair 67, 77a.

72. 22 Mr.] 44, 48, 67, 77a; *omitted* 75, 77b, 79–81, 81, 83.

73. 15 other] 44, 48, 67, 75, 77a, 77b; *omitted* 79–81, 81, 83.

73. 21 Advantage] 48, 67, 77a; Advantages 44, 75, 77b, 79–81, 81, 83.

74. 7 follow] 48, 67, 77a; to follow 44, 75, 77b, 79–81, 81, 83.

75. 15   and] *GM.* 37. 113–14, 44, 48, 67, 77a; or 75, 77b, 79–81, 81, 83.

75. 18   Necessaries] 44, 48, 67, 75, 77a, 77b; necessities 79–81, 81, 83.

76. 3   *Laureat.*] 44, 48, 67, 77a, 79–81, 81, 83; *Laureat*/* **Vol. II. p. 220. 75, 77b.

76. 6   intire] 44, 48, 67, 75, 77a, 77b, 79–81; intire*/*The poem is inserted in the late collection. 81, 83.

76. 11   viz.] *GM.* 38. 210; *omitted* 44, 48, 67, 75, 77a, 77b, 79–81, 81, 83.

76. 17   following Verses] *GM.* 38. 210, 44, 48, 67, 77a; before-mentioned poem*/*Vol. II. p. 220. 75, 77b; before-mentioned poem 79–81, 81, 83.

76. 17   were] *GM.* 38. 210, 44, 48, 67, 75, 77a, 77b; was 79–81, 81, 83.

76. 18   them] *GM.* 38. 210, 44, 48, 67, 75, 77a, 77b; it 79–81, 81, 83.

76. 24   Lord] 44, 48, 67, 75, 77b, 79–81, 81, 83; Lords 77a.

77. 6   Your's *&c.*] 44, 48, 67, 75, 77a, 77b, 79–81, 81, 83; Your's, T. B. *GM.* 38. 210.

77. 7 ff.   *poem*] 44, 48, 67, 77a; *omitted* 75, 77b, 79–81, 81, 83.

77. 7   Laureat.] 44, 48, 67, 77a; LAUREAT, Nº I. *GM.* 38. 210.

78. 15   your] *GM.* 38. 210, 44, 48; the 67, 77a.

78. 37   whilst] *GM.* 38. 210; while 44, 48, 67, 77a.

81. 6   Poem] 44, 48, 67, 77a; Poem*/*Vol. II. p. 192. 75, 77b; poem*/*Printed in this volume. 79–81; poem*/*Printed in the late collection. 81, 83.

81. 28   Rebellion] 44, 48, 67, 75, 77a, 79–81, 81, 83; a Rebellion 77b.

81. 30   supported him] 44, 48, 75, 77b, 79–81, 81, 83; supported 67, 77a.

83. 5   Ardour] 67, 77a; great Ardour 44, 48, 75, 77b, 79–81, 81, 83.

83. 30   *Divine*] 44, 48, 67, 77a, 79–81, 81, 83; DIVINE*/* Vol. II. p. 111. 75, 77b.

84. 4   of] 44, 48, 75, 77b, 79–81, 81, 83; in 67, 77a.

84. 10   it] 48, 67, 75, 77a, 77b, 79–81, 81, 83; *omitted* 44.

84. 17   a] 48, 67, 77a; *omitted* 44, 75, 77b, 79–81, 81, 83.

84. 22   *Savage*] 44, 48, 67, 75, 77a, 77b, 79–81, 81, 83; S——e *WM*.

84. 23   he spent] 44, 48, 67, 75, 77a, 77b, 79–81, 81, 83; he'd spend *WM*.

84. 24   and Fasting] 44, 48, 67, 75, 77a, 77b, 79–81, 81, 83; in Fasting *WM*.

86. 14   their] 44, 48, 75, 77b, 79–81, 81, 83; the 67, 77a.

86. 19   he made] 44, 48, 75, 77b, 79–81, 81, 83; he had made 67, 77a.

87. 18   Want] 44, 48, 75, 77b, 79–81, 81, 83; the Want 67, 77a.

88. 14 ff. *footnote*] 44, 48, 67, 77a; *replaced by* Vol. II. p. 173. 75, 77b; *omitted* 79–81, 81, 83.

89. 22 ff. *footnote*] 44, 48, 67, 77a; replaced by Ibid. p. 202. 75, 77b; *omitted* 79–81, 81, 83.

90. 10   feign'd] *GM*. 41. 491; fam'd 44, 48, 67, 77a.

90. 32   thin] *GM*. 41. 491; then 44, 48, 67, 77a.

91. 5   greatest] 44, 48, 67, 75, 77a, 77b; highest 79–81, 81, 83.

91. 29   though] *GM*. 41. 491; through 44, 48, 67, 77a.

92. 35   be] 44, 48, 67, 75, 77a, 77b, 79–81; *omitted* 81, 83.

93. 21 ff. *footnote*] 44, 48, 67, 77a; *replaced by* Vol. II. p. 141. 75, 77b; *omitted* 79–81, 81, 83.

94. 26   what] *PS*, 44; what's 48, 67, 77a.

94. 28   Gates] 44, 48, 67, 77a; Doors *PS*.

96. 22   received] 44, 75, 77b, 79–81, 81, 83; receive 48, 67, 77a.

97. 7   no] 48, 67, 77a; not 44, 75, 77b, 79–81, 81, 83.

97. 17   the Man] 44, 48, 75, 77b, 79–81, 81, 83; A Man 67, 77a.

97. 23   be imagined but that] 48, 67, 77a; be imagined that 44, 75, 77b; but be imagined that 79–81, 81, 83.

97. 27   Fortitude] 44, 48, 67, 77a; Happiness *W*, 75, 77b,
          79–81, 81, 83.

97. 30   Or amidst Woes] 44, 48, 67, 77a; If amidst Woe *W*,
          75, 77b, 79–81, 81, 83.

97. 31   **mean Acts**] **44, 48, 67, 77a**; low Arts *W*, 75, 77b,
          79–81, 81, 83.

98. 22   his Distresses] 44, 48, 67, 77a; distresses 75, 77b, 79–81,
          81, 83.

98. 29   nor] 48, 67, 77a; and 44, 75, 77b, 79–81, 81, 83.

98. 30   he] 48, 67, 77a; not 44, 75, 77b, 79–81, 81, 83.

98. 30–1 Difficulty] 67, 77a; equal Difficulty 44, 48, 75, 77b,
          79–81, 81, 83.

99. 21   the] 48; that 44, 75, 77b; upon the 67, 77a; on that
          79–81, 81, 83.

100. 9   Condition] 48, 67, 77a; Fortune 44, 75, 77b, 79–81,
          81, 83.

100. 12   Wealth] 48, 67, 77a; Affluence 44, 75, 77b, 79–81,
          81, 83.

102. 18   was] 48, 67, 77a; he was 44, 75, 77b, 79–81, 81, 83.

103. 30   as long] 44, 48, 67, 77a; as long as 75, 77b, 79–81,
          81, 83.

104. 2   Fear] 44, 48, 67, 75, 77a, 77b; the fear 79–81, 81, 83.

104. 5   Corners. But] 44, 48, 75, 77b, 79–81, 81, 83; Corners,
          but 67, 77a.

104. 29   to amuse] 44, 48, 67, 77a; or amuse 75, 77b, 79–81,
          81, 83.

105. 7   had] 44, 48, 67, 77a; *omitted* 75, 77b, 79–81, 81, 83.

106. 23–4 Genius. [*new paragraph*] He] 48, 67, 77a; Genius.
          He 44, 75, 77b, 79–81, 81, 83.

106. 29   Walk] 44, 48, 75, 77b, 79–81, 81, 83; Way 67, 77a.

107. 9 ff. *footnote*] 44, 48, 67, 77a; *replaced by* Vol. II. p. 227.
          75, 77b; *omitted* 79–81, 81, 83.

108. 30 ff. *footnote*] 44, 48, 67, 77a; *replaced by* Vol. II. p. 129.
          75, 77b; *omitted* 79–81, 81, 83.

108. 32   Bounties] 44, 48, 67, 77a; bounty *GM*. 38. 154.

109. 18   Dedication] 44, 48, 67, 77a, 79–81, 81, 83; Dedication*/*Vol. II. p. 229. 75, 77b.

109. 26   Disappointment] 48, 67, 77a; Disappointments 44, 75, 77b, 79–81, 81, 83.

110. 25   his] 44, 48, 75, 77b, 79–81, 81, 83; this 67, 77a.

112. 5   send to] 44, 48, 67, 77a; send 75, 77b, 79–81, 81, 83.

112. 30   him*/*By Mr. *Pope*.] 75, 77b, 79–81, 81, 83; him 44, 48, 67, 77a.

113. 35   that] 67, 77a; which 75, 77b, 79–81, 81, 83; *omitted* 44, 48.

115. 12   all] 48, 67, 77a; *omitted* 44, 75, 77b, 79–81, 81, 83.

116. 6   *Powel*] 44, 48, 67, 77a, 79–81, 81, 83; Powel*/* Vol. II. p. 217. 75, 77b.

116. 7   *Jones*] 44, 48, 67, 77a, 79–81, 81, 83; Jones‡/‡Ibid. p. 197. 75, 77b.

116. 8   *Magazine*] 44, 48, 67, 75, 77a, 77b; MAGAZINE*/*Reprinted in this volume. 79–81, *Magazine*/*Reprinted in the late collection. 81, 83.

116. 23   *Labours*] 44, 48, 75, 79–81, 81, 83; Labour 67, 77a, 77b.

117. 28   had] 48, 67, 77a; *omitted* 44, 75, 77b, 79–81, 81, 83.

117. 28   his] 83; this 44, 48, 67, 75, 77a, 77b, 79–81, 81.

117. 32   that] 44, 48, 67, 77a; *omitted* 75, 77b, 79–81, 81, 83.

118. 34   was] 44, 48, 75, 77b, 79–81, 81, 83; were 67, 77a.

119. 24   still have] 44, 48, 75, 77b, 79–81, 81, 83; have still 67, 77a.

120. 12   fifty] 48, 67, 77a; five 44, 75, 77b, 79–81, 81, 83.

122. 9–10 Weakness) of my Pocket,] 75, 77b, 79–81, 81, 83; Weakness of my Pocket) 44, 48, 67, 77a.

122. 11   'twas] 44, 48; it was 67, 75, 77a, 77b, 79–81, 81, 83.

122. 27   would] 44, 48, 67, 75, 77a, 77b; I would 79–81, 81, 83.

124. 22   been before] 44, 48, 67, 75, 77a, 77b, 79–81, before
         been 81, 83.

124. 25   *that*] 44, 48, 67, 75, 77a, 77b; *omitted* 79–81, 81, 83.

124. 30   *footnote*] 44, 48, 67, 75, 77a, 77b; *omitted* 79–81,
         81, 83.

124. 31   *footnote*] 44, 48, 67, 77a; *replaced by* Letter January
         15. 75, 77b; *omitted* 79–81, 81, 83.

125. 9   a] 75, 77b, 79–81, 81, 83; an 44, 48, 67, 77a.

125. 15   *Jan.* 30th] 44, 48; *January* 30, 67, 77a; January the
         30th 75, 77b, 79–81, 81, 83.

125. 18   Sev'n-night] 44, 48, 67, 77a; se'en-night 75, 77b,
         79–81, 81, 83.

126. 4   constitute] 48, 67, 77a; constituted 44, 75, 77b, 79–81,
         81, 83.

126. 5   cannot] 48, 67, 75, 77a, 77b, 79–81, 81, 83; it cannot
         44.

126. 6   but it was too manifest that] 48, 67, 77a; and indeed
         44, 75, 77b, 79–81, 81, 83.

126. 15   the] 44, 48, 67, 77a; *omitted* 75, 77b, 79–81, 81, 83.

126. 19   tho'] 48, 67, 77a, 79–81, 81, 83; but 44, 75, 77b.

127. 16   the following Poem] 44, 48, 67, 77a; a poem called
         'London and Bristol* delineated.'/*Vol. II. p. 231.
         75, 77b; a poem called 'London and Bristol de-
         lineated.' 79–81, 81, 83.

127. 17 ff. *text of poem*] 44, 48, 67, 77a; *omitted* 75, 77b, 79–81,
         81, 83.

130. 35–6 *See Gentleman's Magazine.* Vol. xiii. p. 496.] 44, 48;
         omitted 67, 77a.

132. 16   publish] 44, 48, 67, 77a, 81, 83; published 75, 77b,
         79–81.

132. 30   Assistances] 48, 67, 77a; Assistance 44, 75, 77b, 79–81,
         81, 83.

133. 17   Offices] 44, 48, 67, 75, 77a, 77b, 79–81; office 81, 83.

134. 5   Prisoner] 48, 67, 77b; a Prisoner 44, 75, 77b, 79–81,
81, 83.

134. 10   Friends*/*Mr. *Pope.*] 75, 77b, 79–81, 81, 83; Friends
44, 48, 67, 77a.

135. 4–5 dictated. Mr. *Savage*] 44, 48, 67, 75, 77a, 77b, 79–81,
81; dictated. Henley, in one of his advertisements,
had mentioned *Pope's treatment of Savage*. This
was supposed by Pope to be the consequence of a
complaint made by Savage to Henley, and was
therefore mentioned by him with much resentment. Mr. Savage 83. See Textual Introduction,
p. xxxv.

135. 13   31st, 1743] 83; 31st 44, 48, 67, 77a; 31st‡/‡In 1743.
75, 77b, 79–81, 81.

135. 21   were] 44, 48, 75, 77b, 79–81, 81, 83; was 67, 77a.

136. 5   his Apprehension] 44, 48, 75, 77b, 79–81, 81, 83; and
his Apprehension 67, 77a.

136. 24   others in their Closets] 83; others in Studies 44, 48,
67, 77a; others in Libraries ms.; in other studies
75, 77b, 79–81, 81.

137. 10   was] 44, 48, 75, 77b, 79–81, 81, 83; used 67, 77a.

137. 30–1 him. *new paragraph* His] 44, 48, 67, 75, 77a, 77b;
him. His 79–81, 81, 83.

138. 5–6 and very small Offences were sufficient to provoke
him] 44, 48, 67, 75, 77a, 77b; (and very small
offences were sufficient to provoke him) 79–81,
81, 83.

138. 11   discharged] 48, 67, 77a; as discharged 44, 75, 77b,
79–81, 81, 83.

138. 22   begun] 75, 77b, 79–81, 81, 83; began 44, 48, 67, 77a.

139. 21   Work] 83; Writer 44, 48, 67, 75, 77a, 77b, 79–81, 81.

139. 30   the] 48, 67, 77a; its 44, 75, 77b, 79–81, 81, 83.

140. 10   surely may be readily] 48, 67, 77a; may surely readily
be 44, 75, 77b, 79–81, 81, 83.

140. 11   than] 44, 48, 67, 75, 77b, 79–81, 81, 83; that 77a.

140. 14   Plenty] 83; Affluence 44, 75, 77b, 79–81, 81; Abundance 48, 67, 77a.

140. 15   a] 48, 67, 77a; any 44, 75, 77b, 79–81, 81, 83.

140. 15   easily] 48, 67, 77a; *omitted* 44, 75, 77b, 79–81, 81, 83.

140. 22   if] 48, 67, 77a; *omitted* 44, 75, 77b, 79–81, 81, 83.

INDEX

Entries marked 'n.' refer to the editor's notes, and not to Johnson's,
which are treated as part of the text.

INDEX

Page, Francis, xiv, 34-5 and n., 40, 41.

Percy Letters, The, 5 n.

Plain Dealer, The, see Hill, Aaron.

Poetical Register, The, see Jacob, Giles.

Pope, Alexander, xiii, xxix–xxxi, xxxii–xxxiii, xxxv, 32 n., 47 n., 48, 50, 51, 53, 100 n., 103 n., 110 n., 112 and n., 114 n., 115 n., 116 n., 133 n., 134 and n.; his *Correspondence* (ed. George Sherburn), 110 n., 115 n., 116 n., 120 n., 133 n., 135 n.; his *Dunciad,* xxix, xxxiii, 46, 48, 49, 50; his *Epigram on Dennis,* 50-1 and n.

Potter, Robert, his *Art of Criticism,* xxvi and n.

Powell, John, 116 and n.

Price, Mr., 126 n.

Prince of Wales, 90, 91 n., 95, 109.

Proceedings at Justice Hall, The, xv.

Queen Caroline, xix, 37-8, 76-7, 79, 80, 81, 86, 87, 89 n., 102, 103 n., 105 and n., 109.

Read, Mrs., 121 n., 122, 133 n.

Rivers, Richard Savage, Earl, 4 and n., 5, 7 n., 8, 9 n., 27.

Rochester, Laurence Hyde, Earl of, 5.

Ruffhead, Owen, his *Life of Pope,* 133 n.

Rundle, Thomas, 83, 84 n.

Rutland, Duchess Dowager of, 26.

Rutland, Duchess of, 26.

Rutland, Duke of, 26.

Salmon, Thomas, his *Review of the History of England,* 4 n., 5.

Saunders, Samuel, 122 n.

Saunders, William, 121 n., 123 n.

Saunders, Mrs. William, 122.

Savage, John, 26.

Savage, Richard (*see also* Smith, Richard, and Surridge, Richard), the anonymous *Life* of, see *Life of Mr. Richard Savage* (1727); his

works: *Author to be Let, An,* xxvii, xxxiii, 8, 45, 46, 67; *Bastard, The,* xii, xxxii, 42-3 and n., 44 n., 70-2 and n., 75, 77 n.; *Convocation, The,* 13 n.; *Epigram on John Dennis,* 51 n.; *Epistles upon Authors,* 41, 89 and n.; *Friend, The,* 22; *Genius of Liberty, The,* 81 n.; *Lampoon against Miller,* 100; *London and Bristol Delineated,* xiv, xxvii, 127-32 and n.; *Love in a Veil,* 13 and n.; *Miscellaneous Poems* (also referred to as his *Miscellany* or *Miscellanies*), xv, xxvii, 9 and n., 10 and n., 25-9 and n., 44 n., 94; *Of Public Spirit in Regard to Public Works,* xxvii, 91-6 and n.; *On False Historians,* 89; *On the Departure of the Prince and Princess of Orange,* see *Genius of Liberty, The; Poem on the Birthday of the Prince of Wales,* see *Of Public Spirit in Regard to Public Works; Poem Sacred to the . . . Memory of . . . King George,* 30; *Poet's Dependance on a Statesman, A,* 88; *Progress of a Divine, The,* 82 n., 83-4 and n., 86; 'Progress of a Freethinker, The', 86; *Religion and Liberty: An Epistle to . . . Sir Robert Walpole,* 51; *Sir Thomas Overbury,* 21-4 and n., 105-6, 110, 116, 119, 125; *To a young Gentleman, a Painter,* 26 n., 94 n.; *Triumph of Health and Mirth, The,* 62-3; *Valentine's Day,* 116 n.; *Volunteer Laureat, The,* 76-81, 102, 106-8 and n., 127 n.; *Wanderer, The,* xxvii, xxviii, 8, 19, 44 n., 52-9 and n., 61-2, 97, 138; *Works* (1775 and 1777), xxii–xxiii, xxxi–xxxiv, 80 n.

Select Trials for Murders at the Session-House in the Old Bailey, xvi, 30 n., 36 n., 38 n.

Sherburn, George, see Pope, Alexander, his *Correspondence.*

Sinclair, James, 31-2 and n., 33, 71.

Smith, Mr., 17.

PRINTED IN GREAT BRITAIN
AT THE UNIVERSITY PRESS, OXFORD
BY VIVIAN RIDLER
PRINTER TO THE UNIVERSITY

Date Due